How to Stop Overthinking

The Art of Creating Problems that Don't Exist

CU01508385

by N

www.NickTrenton.com

Table of Contents

Chapter 1. Your Anxiety Management Toolkit

What does stress look like in your life? More importantly, what effects does it have on you? Most of us use this word "stress" to describe a range of experiences of different kinds and intensities, but one thing is clear: stress almost always *costs* us something. Whether that cost is big or small, obvious or not-so-obvious, the fact is that stress takes a physical, mental, and emotional toll on us.

Whether stress is just an occasional occurrence for you or you're battling a more entrenched anxiety disorder, there are thankfully countless scientifically proven methods for cultivating a calmer, happier, and more balanced life. We'll start this chapter with a few key strategies that will help you understand your anxiety so you can consciously take control.

The first step is always to become aware of where we stand. This means taking a clear, honest look at what anxiety and stress looks like for us, and how it functions in our life. Only then can we start to challenge our beliefs, put labels on our experiences, and start to pick apart the stress response as it plays out in our day-to-day lives. Let's dive in.

1. LABEL YOUR EMOTIONS

When you're stuck in an anxiety spiral, it can be hard to even put a finger on what's happening to you. All you know is one thing: it feels bad! Your thoughts are racing all over the place, and you may even feel physically ill. It's like overthinking, worry, and anxiety are an overwhelming flood that completely washes over you, and you can't escape or defend yourself.

Think about the last time you felt completely swamped with anxiety and overthinking— what did it feel like? If you find it difficult to find the right words to describe the intense feelings, then this following tip will help you.

Dan Siegel is a professor at the UCLA School of Medicine, and teaches people how to "name it and tame it." According to Siegel, when we label our strong emotions, we create distance between us and them. Giving how we feel a name is one way we can almost step outside of that flood of anxiety, rather than being swallowed up by it!

It's a question of controlling your feelings or allowing yourself to be controlled by them. Or a handy way to think of it is: if you can *see* an emotion, you don't have to *be* an emotion.

Psychological distance is the feeling of perspective we gain over our ourselves. The thing is, when we're caught in an overthinking loop or anxious rumination, we lack awareness. We may feel a rush of strong negative emotions, but we lack perspective or the ability to say, "I'm experiencing some anxiety right now."

Much of our fear comes from our inbuilt fight-or-flight response instilled in us by evolution. Based in the amygdala of the brain, this reaction is completely unconscious, automatic, and physiological. To step out of this instinctual, knee-jerk response, we need to pause long enough to realize that we are actually having that response in the first place, and this realization brings us into our "higher brain," the prefrontal cortex.

Clinical psychologist Dr. Mitch Abblett explains how strong emotions like anxiety can be like a hand held right in front of our faces. We are so fixated on that hand that we cannot see anything else in front of us. You can completely lose sight of the fact that the hand is temporary and can be moved. You can lose sight of the fact that there is something *beyond* the hand. Most interesting of all, you may completely lose sight of the fact that the hand is your own, and can be moved away at will – if only you have the presence of mind to do so.

Simply acknowledging what is going on by giving a label to your emotions, however, reminds you that this hand in front of your face wasn't always there, and that it won't be there forever. When you do this, something special happens: you create a little gap in which you get to choose what you do next. It is as though there is a small moment of relief created when you can *say* out loud, "I feel like I'm drowning."

The mere fact of you being able to observe and notice this feeling at all seems to suggest that there is a part of you that is not, in fact, drowning. Suddenly, there is the possibility of another point of view; of someone standing outside that experience and observing the drowning from a distance. The immediate result is often relief. So what's going on here?

Matthew Lieberman and colleagues published a paper in *Psychological Science* back in 2007, where they found that "affect labeling" (i.e., putting feelings into words) actually alters the brain. When Liberman's test subjects underwent fMRI scans while experiencing strong emotions, simply labeling these emotions decreased activity in all the regions of the brain associated with emotional regulation, particularly the amygdala. *This* is the little gap. Once the strong emotional response is dampened, then we can go in and allow our rational brains to step in and solve problems for us.

This is the lesson that mindfulness practitioners have been teaching for years. When we label an emotion, it is no longer something we *are,* but something we *are aware of.* And so we disengage. And when that strong anxiety is not so firmly attached to us, we can make decisions from a calmer, more deliberate place psychologically.

How do we name emotions as we're experiencing them? It can be difficult in the heat of the moment, but that's exactly when we need to learn to do it! Here's a step-by-step guide:

- First, simply become aware of what your *body* is doing. Your body is in the moment and will be the first to alert you to strong emotions. Let's say you've just gotten off the phone with your father, and a few minutes later, you become aware of an awful, antsy feeling around your shoulders and chest and a horrible, tight lump in the back of your throat.
- When you notice this physical response, stop. Just pause and bring awareness to it. Let's say you excuse yourself and go and sit quietly in your room for a moment.
- Next, breathe a little more slowly and focus on the physical sensation while you try to identify what you're feeling. You are only looking for a label—not an accusation, diagnosis, or judgment. Maybe after a few breaths, you say to yourself out loud, "I am feeling anxiety . . . I'm having worried and panicky thoughts . . ."
- At this point, you can literally imagine the word "anxiety" as separate from you. Visualize the word "anxiety" in letters that you hold in your hands or which you can pin to your clothing.
- Keep breathing and notice how you feel after you give your experience a name.

Here, you might be wondering if you need to get away from the anxiety, or somehow visualize yourself destroying it. But you don't! Simple awareness is enough to create distance. You don't have to fight with what you feel, or analyze it, or rush to find a solution. You just need to be aware and feel what you feel.

Before any meaningful action can take place, you need to be able to see what you're feeling. So just focus on that for a moment. Try not to say, "I am stressed." *You* are not stressed, you're just you, and you're experiencing stress. There is stress. Stress is occurring. As you breathe in and out, try simply saying "stress." Once you can identify the phenomenon unfolding, you can see that it is not especially attached to you . . . if you don't want it to be. It is just something that is happening.

Sometimes with anxiety we can get caught in a trap, feeling anxious about how anxious we feel. So, for this exercise, don't fight anything. Our awareness is not a "solution" to anything; it's simply an emergency stop on a runaway thought process. It allows us to gently remove the hand from in front of our face.

2. BUILD SELF-AWARENESS

To be able to label our emotions and to question our beliefs and thoughts, there is one thing we cannot do without: self-awareness. Anxious rumination can *feel* like we're thinking, like we're being aware, but it's usually an illusion. We're not really solving any problems, clarifying the situation, or getting anywhere—we're just going round in circles and making ourselves feel bad.

To give you an example, think about someone who suffers from the all-too-common "health anxiety." Such a person may spend many unhappy hours Googling vague symptoms and investigating scary-sounding illnesses that they're certain they have. They battle constantly with the thought that they are very, very ill and maybe even about to die.

If you ask this person what the problem is, they will say, "I have a complicated case of Ribose-5-Phosphate Isomerase Deficiency, and this cramp in my arm is actually an ongoing seizure, I'm convinced of it. But I can't get any of the doctors to take me seriously..."

You can see, however, that this is not the real problem. With more self-awareness, the person could instead say, "When I'm tired or run-down, I tend to get hyper-focused on bodily sensations and then get carried away with researching symptoms and self-diagnosing. I know that it's health anxiety, though, and that I'm not really sick."

Self-awareness is like an escape hatch out of an anxiety spiral, and it's *not* the same thing as just being more anxious!

A moment of self-awareness in the midst of an anxiety spiral can be a life raft, but it also pays to cultivate an overall greater sense of self-awareness in everyday life. It's almost as though you're inoculating yourself against runaway thoughts in the future. Self-awareness is not just a skill, but a stable, long-term trait. It is about knowing and understanding yourself, including your strengths, weaknesses, triggers, and joys.

Greater self-awareness is not some abstract quality. It results in real self-esteem, greater calm, and a more internal focus of control (i.e., the feeling that *you* are in charge and not merely reacting to outside forces).

Here are three practical tips to try in order to deepen your self-awareness.

Tip 1: Keep a thought diary

This an easy, accessible way to constantly monitor/tune into your feelings and plans. Eventually, you internalize the ability to notice what you're feeling without pausing to put pen to paper. When you write your thoughts down, you practice labeling and the distance it brings. You also see your own self-talk more clearly; what effect does it have on you to think these thoughts? When you're flustered, sit down and pour everything onto the page. But rather than ruminating, use the journal to go on a fact-finding mission.

How are you feeling? What came before these feelings? What are you thinking? What is in your control here and what isn't? How accurate are your appraisals? What resources do you have right now? What are you trying to achieve and is your approach working? What action can you take?

You'll know a journaling session has been successful when you close the pages and feel like you've reached an end and gained some insight into where to go next. One tip: focus on the *what* rather than the *why*.

Tip 2: Engage in mindfulness practices

You don't need to have a full-blown yoga practice or a daily meditation session to benefit from mindfulness. Remember, the key is to gain awareness—and even a moment of awareness can bring distance, control, and a sense of relief from overthinking.

Practice strengthening the body-mind connection by doing some deep breathing and stretching exercises, or spend some time in quiet contemplation. The only goal is to stay present in your body, in your breath, and in the moment. You are not trying to accomplish anything, play "gotcha!" with your thoughts, or judge how mindful you're being. Try to aim for a few seconds of still, calm awareness peppered all throughout the day whenever you can remember.

Tip 3: Take a personal inventory

When trapped in anxious overthinking, your mind can convince you that everything is awful and that you're completely hopeless. But the truth is that you have many strengths, skills, and resources at your disposal. You always have options. Beyond that, you can strengthen your self-esteem by frankly acknowledging your limitations and weaknesses. When you're aware of your flaws, you can own them.

There are many ways to learn more about yourself and what makes you tick—good and bad. An easy example is to simply acknowledge the fact that you have a tendency to ruminate. If you know this about yourself, then you're instantly empowered to work around these limitations. You're never caught off guard, unaware of why you do what you do. You recognize your triggers when they emerge, and you know the ways to manage them.

You could take psychometric tests or do self-assessments like the MBTI, which will help you better understand your personality. You could also ask those closest to you to share what they understand about your strengths and weaknesses as people looking from the outside in. One interesting exercise is to make a list of what you think your ten best and worst traits are (for example, "dedicated" or "aloof") and then compare them to a list you ask a close friend or family member to compile. You may be surprised!

Alternatively, ask mentors or work colleagues to give you (considerate) feedback to help you better appreciate aspects of your behavior you might not see clearly. A therapist is another person who can help you gain a clear, balanced, and accurate view of yourself that can help moderate the tendency to overthink.

One big caveat about self-awareness and introspection, however, we do not necessarily gain any self-awareness by simply turning inward and contemplating our navels. There is, in fact, a wrong way to be self-aware! It's easy to imagine why-you only replicate any bias or blind spots you have, and never get to test your theories against reality.

There are actually *two* kinds of self-awareness—internal and external. The former is about how well we know our own needs, goals, and feelings, and the latter is about understanding how others see us. Introspection typically only helps us with internal self-awareness, but we need *both* types to be balanced, well-functioning people.

Simply being aware of what we think and feel doesn't mean that these thoughts or feelings are right or helpful. In fact, research by organizational psychologist Tasha Eurich has shown that people who introspect a lot may actually be *worse* at self-awareness! Seeing that ninety-five percent of people claim to be self-aware when just fifteen percent are, Eurich said that "eighty percent of us are lying to ourselves about whether we're lying to ourselves."

Anxiety and overthinking thrive in the private spaces in our own minds. If we can open up those spaces, shine some light on them, and invite in others' perspectives to moderate our own, we can reshape the thought patterns that cause us anxiety.

For example, you could argue with yourself for years about whether people secretly dislike you at work, writing fruitlessly in a diary under the guise of gaining awareness about why you're so unlikable. But if you go out there and gather genuine feedback from your colleagues and discover that you are, in fact, not disliked at all, you gain real, usable self-awareness that will diminish your anxiety, not increase it!

3. QUESTION YOURSELF USING SOCRATIC METHOD

If you suffer from anxiety and overthinking, you can sometimes start to think of your brain as an enemy. You might start to view thinking of any kind as stressful and exhausting. But the truth is, your brain, and the rationality it is capable of, is a wonderful thing. The mind is a terrible master and a wonderful servant, as they say. Borrowing some cognitive tools from the philosopher Socrates can help us train our faculties to work for us rather than against us.

Socrates once said, "I know you won't believe me, but the highest form of human excellence is to question oneself and others." For people who find their ruminating takes on an endless, compulsive quality, questions can act as a clarifier, cutting away at useless rumination and allowing us to see ourselves and our thought processes more clearly.

Using the Socratic method, you will be able to assess the credibility and logic of your own thoughts. This can be a powerful antidote to the illogic of our most anxious obsessions. You will also be able to identify your own thought patterns and recognize inconsistencies and assumptions.

First of all, let's make a distinction:

Here is an anxious question: "What if something goes wrong? What if *everything* goes wrong?"

Here is a more useful question: "What evidence do I have that this is a problem?"

Both are questions, but they act in very different ways. The first one is open-ended, vague, and, actually, when you look closely, cannot have a real answer. This is the kind of question that encourages, you guessed it, more overthinking. The second question, however, is focused, deliberate, and intended to bring clarity. It has an answer. And that answer can be acted upon.

When you practice Socratic questioning, you are emptying your mind and assuming you know nothing, then proceeding methodically and logically. What do you really know? Instead of running away with assumptions, guesses, and foregone conclusions, you *discover* the answer step by step. The usual outcome is that you realize your anxiety was an illusion created by faulty assumptions, not objective reality.

Let's say you do the exercise from the previous section and uncover an anxious thought: "My elderly father is really ill and may not last the rest of the year." This leads to, "He's probably going to die any day now, and I won't be able to cope when it happens . . ."

But if you can open that gap by pausing, you can ask questions. According to Clark & Egen (2015) the Socratic method survives in modern-day psychology in the form of Cognitive Behavioral Therapy, which focuses on examining thoughts and beliefs so they can be consciously modified. A good question can help you untangle thoughts that are creating anxiety for you. A "good question" is concise, open (yet purposeful), curious, and neutral— i.e., there is no judgment or an assumed right answer.

Conventionally, Socratic dialogues (and CBT therapy) take place between two people having a conversation. But with practice, you can have a conversation with yourself, or more accurately, with your anxious thoughts. Let's return to our example and look at a few questions that can help guide us out of confusion and stress:

Clarification questions: What do you mean by "really ill?" What exactly will happen if you "can't cope"?

Questions that challenge assumptions: Do you have reason to believe he will die soon? Are you making assumptions about his illness?

Uncovering evidence: Can you find any proof that death is imminent? Do you have all the information you need to reach that conclusion?

Exploring alternatives: Is it possible that he may, in fact, live? How are his doctors framing his illness?

Exploring implications: What effect is this fear having on your life? How does this impact others?

By asking these questions, the person in our example could soon realize that although his father's illness is serious, there is actually very little evidence to suggest that he will die. He can look again at his original thought: "He's probably going to die any day now and I won't be able to cope when it happens . . ." This thought causes anxiety and launches a whole avalanche of other equally anxious thoughts. But can it be modified?

After gently questioning himself, he can arrive at a milder idea: "There is always a chance that he could die, and that is the case for any of us at any time, but he is alive and well now, and there is absolutely no reason to overthink it." What's more, in the calm that this more balanced idea creates, he could start to see that he actually has very little information and can take action by talking to his father or his father's doctor to better understand the situation rather than passively panicking about it.

When it comes to overthinking, Socratic dialogue can help us slow down and not simply take our own word for it! Your brain can be your worst enemy or your best friend. Commit to using your brainpower for good, and you can actually reduce anxiety by finding clarity and useful ways forward. The next time you've identified a stressful thought in yourself, put it under the microscope and ask it to defend itself. Why should you allow an irrational, inaccurate, or flat-out wrong idea to torment and bother you? Try this process:

Step 1: Put your anxious thoughts or ideas into a sentence.

Step 2: Ask, is there any evidence to believe it? Also ask what you one hundred percent know and what is merely bias, expectation, fear, assumption, exaggeration, or catastrophic thinking.

Step 3: Challenge yourself. If something seems a little shaky, look closer. Deliberately look for alternatives or counterexamples to challenge what you currently think.

Step 4: Rewrite this thought into something more moderate.

Even if you can remember none of these steps in the heat of the moment, just remind yourself to challenge your assumptions, ask questions, and look for evidence. Remember, too, that you don't even have to come to some grand conclusion at all. It is always a possibility that you withhold judgment and choose not to react in the first place–we'll explore this idea more later in the book. For now, it's a wonderful thing to simply decide that you won't grasp hold of a thought until it has stood on trial to justify itself!

4. TEST YOUR FALSE BELIEFS

The funny thing about anxiety is how *unreal* it is. You can convince yourself that something is really a Very Big Problem, but if you look at it with another perspective, all you can see is a person sitting safely and comfortably in their living room, having a series of electro-chemical signals run through their brain. That's literally it. The Very Big Problem is simply a story they're telling themselves.

Imagine someone having a sudden "aha!" moment about their own anxiety. One day, they witness *someone else* having a panic attack. They have experienced these awful episodes themselves countless times, but they have never seen the process unfold from the outside, so to speak.

Observing from the outside in, they cannot help but be struck by an obvious observation: the entire episode is occurring within that person's mind. Inside that mind, the world is ending. *But the world isn't ending.* As you can imagine, this throws light on the observers own experience. The next time they find themselves slipping into an anxious spiral or attack, they have this episode in the back of their mind... for a moment, they are able to see themselves as an observer would see them. The world certainly feels like it's ending... but it isn't.

When we worry and ruminate, we can take any old story and behave *as if it were true*. We can start with "what if they were laughing at me?" and end with "I'm an awful human being and everyone hates me for sure," all with zero correction or input from the objective world around us. The brain has an amazing capacity to entertain thoughts and ideas that simply aren't true. This is an amazing ability that allows us to be creative, to plan, to dream, and to think up new solutions that don't yet exist. But it also allows us to dream up awful hypotheticals and fictitious theories that act like mental torture devices we make for ourselves.

There's one blindingly obvious way to counter this tendency of the brain to run off unchecked into the unreal—test it. Do an experiment. Compare what's in your head with what's out there in the world and see if your anxious model of reality actually stands up to scrutiny. It sounds like an odd way to go about it, but how often have you worked yourself up into a froth over an idea that you never once stopped to check the veracity of? How often have you told yourself a mental story and simply assumed it was true without ever checking to see if it was?

Much research is now focused on revealing the relationship between anxiety disorders, perception, and the inability to tolerate uncertainty. Psychologist Aaron Beck and his colleagues claimed that anxiety "*is an uncontrollable affective response dependent upon the **interpretation** of a situation and the appraisal of a possible threat of negative events*." Basically, the anxiety is not a result of the stimulus itself, but our interpretation of that stimulus as a threat. We decide how anxious we feel based on:

- How likely we think the threat is to occur
- How bad we think it'll be when it happens
- How well we predict we can cope
- How much help we can expect from the outside

As you can see, all of the above are about *perception* of reality, not reality. If we appraise something as a threat (for example, people laughing when we walk into a room), we may respond with a racing heart, a blush, and a flood of negative thoughts, i.e., "they're laughing at me." Almost without knowing you're doing it, you could create a rich inner theory about this experience designed to deal with the perceived threat and uncertainty. Your anxiety, once started, seems to feed on itself so quickly that you never stop to ask, "Are they actually laughing at me?"

Testing our false beliefs can act like a safety valve that breaks the anxiety cycle. For a simple example, you could straight out ask in the moment if people are laughing at you, or pull someone aside and ask them in private what their interpretation of events was. "Oh no, Emma just told a really funny joke the moment you walked in!"

Using Socratic dialogue, too, is a way to test our assumptions before we get carried away with them. True, sometimes you really don't know—but this is where tolerance of uncertainty comes into play. If you have no way of knowing whether people were in fact laughing at you, for example, you could still conclude, "Well, I have no evidence either way." Sometimes, you may have a more vague and general belief, such as, "My whole friend group secretly dislikes me." This belief, too, can be tested.

See if you can ask yourself questions to test this potentially false belief:

- How likely we think the threat is to occur—How likely is it really that people you consider friends all secretly dislike you? Is it really all that possible, given how often they choose to spend time with you?

- How bad we think it'll be when it happens—Even if your friends occasionally didn't get on with you, would that be so bad? Is it the end of the world if someone doesn't like you one hundred percent? Does one person disliking you mean that others won't, or that you're completely unlikable?
- How well we predict we can cope—Is being a little concerned about this really such a big deal? Is it really crucial that you find out how others feel deep down, or can you handle a little ambiguity?
- How much help we can expect from the outside—If you struggle with this idea, isn't it possible you can talk to your friends about how you feel? Could you sort out your feelings with a therapist or someone else you trust?

Another very direct way to test our potentially false beliefs is through **exposure therapy**. Traditionally, psychologists have used this approach to help people overcome specific phobias. The idea is that if you repeatedly expose yourself to a stimulus that you firmly believe you can't tolerate, you show yourself that you *can* tolerate it. You give yourself proof that the thought "I can't get on a plane because I'll crash" is actually not true.

Your brain makes an interpretation of a stimulus and decides that it's a threat. But when you repeatedly encounter this "threat" and nothing bad happens, your brain soon has to adjust its appraisal. This is a very practical way to directly challenge assumptions, because the evidence simply cannot be denied. Eventually, you learn to internalize this updated version of reality, and let go of your distorted idea of that reality.

Importantly, this isn't something that happens abstractly in your head. It's something you **do** out there in the world. The moment you take thoughts and feelings out of your head and externalize them into the world, you allow them to be tested. What is real remains, what is anxious illusion and fantasy disappears like mist.

To make exposure therapy work, however, you have to *tolerate the stimulus until it no longer provokes a fear response.* Quit before this point, and you only reinforce that the stimulus is a bad thing that you need to fear and avoid. Your anxiety may rise in the face of a stimulus, and if you choose to escape at the moment when your anxiety is highest, then that anxiety will naturally fall when you flee the situation. Your brain will register the drop in anxiety, and conclude that escaping was the right thing to do, and that the stimulus really was frightening after all. This is the exact situation you need to take care to avoid when using exposure therapy principles to tackle anxiety.

So, how can you properly use exposure therapy in your own life when dealing with overthinking?

First, identify a thought or story you're telling yourself that is causing you to feel anxious; for example, "I'm incapable of public speaking." Let's say the thought of public speaking causes a major anxiety response.

The next step is to see if this can be tested in reality. Sit down and write a list of graded steps you can take to gradually expose yourself to the idea of public speaking. Remember to tolerate the stimulus until it doesn't cause a fear response anymore.

Maybe you sign up for an amateur acting class and practice, in baby steps, getting on stage and speaking a few lines, then gradually increasing the time you spend on stage. Work up to offering to give a presentation at work where you have to speak for a longer period. Every time you expose yourself to the stimulus, challenge yourself to observe what is happening: is it *really* as bad as you thought? Are you absolutely "incapable," or do you just find it a little unfamiliar and uncomfortable?

Finally, keep going and allow your experiences to gently challenge your original thought. Maybe you eventually arrive at a more balanced view. "I don't really enjoy public speaking, but it's something I can do if I need to, and I'm sure I could get better if I practiced."

Not all beliefs and thoughts can be challenged with exposure therapy. If that's the case for you, try to embrace the uncertainty rather than rush in with a story or theory to help counter the perceived "threat." It can take practice to simply say "I don't know yet what kind of situation this is" instead of "this is a bad situation." The next time you encounter an ambiguous or unresolved situation, choose to deliberately interpret it as *unknown rather than threatening.* "That girl from last night's date hasn't replied to my text. I don't know how she feels about me yet," is far less anxiety-provoking than, "She hasn't replied. She's definitely not interested. I hate dating!"

Researchers are now wondering whether uncertainty intolerance is a kind of personal characteristic or trait that predisposes us to anxiety. Gentes & Ruscio published a meta-analysis in 2011 in *Clinical Psychology Review* exploring this trait in detail, and through statistically analyzing the data, they found definite and significant links between mental illness and what has been called "paralysis of cognition and action in the face of uncertainty."

How well a person can tolerate uncertainty has even been implicated in things like OCD, social anxiety, depression, and even eating disorders, so if this is something you recognize in yourself, learning to tolerate the unknown could make a drastic difference to many areas of your life, stress included.

5. MAKE A MIND MAP

What does anxiety and overthinking *look like*?

Close your eyes right now and visualize how rumination and stress look. If you're like most people, you might imagine one thing: chaos. Maybe you imagine a big overwhelming flood of things running into one another, a noisy jumble, or a riot of things that are moving too fast and without any order or control. For many people, anxious thoughts are often characterized by never-ending loops, knots, tangles, and too many thoughts piled up on top of each other in a complete mess, right?

Knowing this about how anxiety *feels* and *looks*, we can work backwards to untangle those metaphorical knots.

Brain dumping is a seriously useful tool for cutting through this mind clutter and finding sweet, sweet **clarity**. Think of it as an organized brain dump. Instead of letting that plate of crazy mental spaghetti swirl around in your head, you put it down on paper, and see just exactly what you're dealing with, where it starts, and where it ends.

From there, you can start to get some relief, organize things, claim back a little control, solve problems, take action to improve what you can, and let go of those things you can't change.

It's as though you are in a crowded and chaotic train station, running around, getting freaked out about every tiny detail. But when you make a mind map, you zoom out and get a bird's eye view of everything. The train station *isn't* a crazy mess–there's rhyme and reason in the way it's laid out, and it can be made sense of. Suddenly, you don't feel so overwhelmed, and you can also start to see how things can be simplified, decluttered, and slowed down. You can certainly see which stimuli can be completely ignored!

The technique is very simple. First, get out a piece of blank paper and a pen or pencil and sit somewhere you'll be undisturbed for a while. Begin with a focus word or phrase—you don't have to nail down the single Big Issue that's worrying you; just put down the first main problem that springs to mind. Importantly, you don't want to get distracted by doing it "right" or analyzing at this stage. Just give yourself permission to put everything you're thinking of onto the page. Don't overthink it.

For example, you sit down and imagine your head is a jug and you're pouring everything out. The first word that comes out is DEADLINE. You scribble this in dark, menacing letters at the center of the page, then draw some branches around it. On these branches, you explore different aspects of this main nub of anxiety. You could explore, for example:

- How you feel about it
- The people involved
- Physical sensations
- The history of this idea or feeling
- Events in the past
- Thoughts about this idea
- Related areas of concern
- Why it's a problem

- Other complicating factors

From each of these branches, you extend more details. For example, branching from DEADLINE could be "I feel resentful and obliged" and "exhausted" as feelings about an upcoming tight deadline. Off of the "resentful" branch, however, you may discover you have even more mental material to dump, and draw more sub-branches: "I agreed to this when I knew I shouldn't have." This may lead to some other branches to do with your job or boundaries that need strengthening (more on this in a later chapter).

Now for the second part. Once you've put everything down, just pause for a moment and see if there's anything else in there. Remember that you are not in problem-solving, judging, or organizing mode just yet. You are in brain-dump mode. And yes, it will be messy (that's the point!).

How do you organize the mess? Well, take a breath and consciously ask your brain to go into a different mode. When we overthink and ruminate, we are in a state of mind where we are constantly distracted by endless detail and irrelevant minutiae. To get out of anxiety, we need to stop being at the mercy of these meaningless details and start instead to take control of them. Cut through the clutter with these four questions:

- What can I control?
- What can I not control?
- What can I DO to improve my situation?
- What really matters to me most?

When we focus on control, concrete action, and our values, it's as though we have a sword that cuts through mental confusion and overwhelm. Let's go back to our example. You look at the resulting mind map and ask first what you can control. You see that you cannot change the fact of the deadline, or the fact of what you have already done in the past. But you see that you can control what you do right now. You have a look at your mind map and see some patterns (in previous maps you might have made, too.)

You keep turning these questions over and over again, and the issue begins to take a simpler, clearer shape. It seems that every time you agree to act against your own principles or values, and any time you take on the work you think you should be doing rather than the work you can realistically do, then you feel stressed and resentful. Still, what to actually do with this insight? Well, you can make sure you act differently next time. But what about now?

Perhaps you take a yellow highlighter and highlight only those parts of the mind map that you can reasonably do anything about. When you are literally staring at a page of clutter with only one or two yellow lines through it, you can see for yourself how much of your thoughts are useful, and how much is pure distraction, stress, and overthinking!

It sounds too simple, but sometimes, if we can visually see how much of our stress is unnecessary, we can more easily let it go. The stressed mind loves vague, general visions of doom. But if you can narrow things down to specifics, put words to them, and start ordering your thoughts, you start to see how insignificant most of your thought traffic actually is. The giant plate of spaghetti, you realize, is really just *one* long noodle that's gotten a bit twisted!

Mind mapping takes a little practice. You have plenty of liberty to adjust this tool as required until it works for you and your life. Just be careful that you don't inadvertently give yourself another tool for rumination!

If you're feeling overwhelmed, simply go back to the four questions above. If you feel a little lost, look for patterns. For example, even though it feels like you have three dozen separate things to worry about, could they really all be versions of the same thing? And if you're feeling bad, try to find specific words to describe it. "Everything is wrong and I hate my life" is so big and overwhelming, but "I am overwhelmed right now by the number of tasks I feel people expect me to do" is smaller and more manageable.

You may carry on even further with your mind map exercise and eventually whittle the problem down to, "I actually have just two things I need to do now. It *feels* like two thousand things, but when I write them down, I see that I don't actually have too many tasks on my plate."

Once you've gotten the hang of mind maps for stress management, you can incorporate other techniques covered in this book. For example, you can use a mind map to help you identify false beliefs you want to rewrite, ask questions of yourself, or put labels on the emotions you're feeling. You can also use a mind map in more practical, everyday ways, for example to order and organize schedules, tasks, lists, and plans. Sometimes, trying to hold such mundane things in your head is itself stressful; put it all down on paper and walk away from it all for a while. When you come back, you may find that the whole thing looks a lot less intimidating.

Finally, it's worth remembering that sometimes, a mind map alone won't magically solve all your problems or shine a light out of a dilemma. But what it will always do is put you in a proactive, rational, and conscious frame of mind. And *this* will make you feel calmer and more in control, whether you solve the problem or not!

6. PLAY MIND GAMES

One powerful weapon we have against useless overthinking is distraction, or, as T.S. Eliot phrased it, "distracted from distraction by distraction." Here's the thing: if you already know logically that your rumination does not serve you in any way, then you know you can safely ignore it.

Fighting with overwhelming thoughts just makes them stronger. What you need instead is a complete break and to completely take your mind off things. Being distracted is sometimes the perfect (and only!) way to short circuit rumination and give yourself enough of a break to gain mental serenity again.

Yes, "distraction" has a bad reputation. But if we use it consciously and deliberately, it can be a way to quickly escape a runaway brain when things like mindfulness are just not going to work.

Playing "mind games" with yourself is a little like catching an unhappy child's attention by waving a stuffed toy around. You can't rationalize with a two-year-old having a tantrum about something that makes no sense in the first place. All you can do is cleverly pull attention away long enough to get them to calm down! Think of your anxious brain the same way—it's just a child having a tantrum. It's just gotten stuck in the mud and needs a quick shove to loosen it again. Here are a few ideas to help you do just that:

Game 1: Fantasize about the perfect day

If there were absolutely nothing to stop you, what would your perfect day look like? If you had all the money, time, and energy in the world, what would you get up to from the moment you opened your eyes in the morning? Have fun with it. If you like, you can construct your own imaginary hypothetical society, or dream up the perfect home—it doesn't have to be realistic or make any sense. It just has to be entertaining.

Game 2: Get lost in questions

Anxiety and curiosity are mutually exclusive experiences—you cannot be both at the same time.

Imagine you're a child again and looking at the world with completely fresh eyes. What stands out to you? What's really weird when you start thinking about it? What have you always secretly wondered, but never actually investigated?

You don't have to come up with any profound insights or do anything to find out the answers to big questions. Just playing around with being open and loose. Like, who decided where the borders of countries go? What was it like when there were no "countries"? When was the first time they even used that word? Has there ever been someone born exactly on a boundary?

Game 3: Go on a mental walk

One sneaky way to distract yourself is simply to give your poor overworked brain a job that is pretty simple yet engrossing. You can "displace" anxious thoughts with neutral or pleasant ones that require your full attention.

Close your eyes and picture a favorite place, a holiday you've gone on, or a well-known route you've traveled in the past. Now mentally walk through this visualization, taking plenty of time to flesh out the details on each of the five senses. See how much you can remember from your childhood home or classroom. Or try to reconstruct the layout of the supermarket you used to go to in another town. This is a great exercise when you're trying to fall asleep.

Game 4: The alphabet game

This one is simple. Pick a broad category, like animals, food, or movies, then move through the alphabet thinking of an item that starts with that letter. For example, "aardvark, baboon, camel, dinosaur . . ."

You could make yourself think of three items before moving on, or make a special rule where you can avoid tricky letters like Q, if you want to. Or, when you get to Z, go around the alphabet again and repeat the process with new items.

Game 5: Build your mental museum

This is a little like going on a mental walk, except instead of fleshing out a memory you already have, you build something from scratch. Start by imagining that you're in a completely empty room with bare white walls—or go a step further and imagine no walls at all (remember that scene in *The Matrix*?). Now assemble a collection of things exactly as you want them.

Maybe you could gather up a few favorite images or paintings, or make an exhibition of all your favorite items—or, for that matter, your favorite people! Collect little mementos that remind you of happy memories or of things you care about. You can make the theme of the museum anything you like. It can be personal or simply a fantastical vision of a hypothetical museum you'd love to visit.

Game 6: Memory game

Give your brain the task of remembering a speech, poem, pattern, or sequence. Challenge yourself. You could also play counting games where you count backward or skip ahead in fixed intervals—or go backward in fixed intervals!

Game 7: People watch

If you're feeling anxious when away from home and need a distraction in a public place, try people watching. Watch people walk by and try to guess their names, their occupations, their ages, or even their deepest secrets. See if you can imagine what each person is thinking at that very moment, or where they may be headed to.

It's true that distraction can be harmful if done compulsively or unconsciously, but it can certainly be a clever way to manage stress if used wisely. You can even try inventing your own distraction games. The only aim is to find a mental activity that is absorbing enough to pull your mind away from compulsive rumination. The idea is that once you've played the game for a while, you'll come back to the "real world" and discover you're feeling much more relaxed.

7. USE THE ABC MODEL TO UNDERSTAND YOUR STRESS

You're probably beginning to notice a few themes here. It seems that for all methods for tackling anxiety, we need to do the opposite of what our stressed and ruminative mind wants us to do!

For example, where it wants to be general and vague, we can be specific.

Where it wants to jump to conclusions, we can slow down and look at the facts.

Where it wants to be irrational and panicky, we can be deliberate, conscious, and in control.

One great framework for understanding a whole range of approaches to stress reduction is called the ABC model. It pulls you out of the reactive, unconscious frame of mind that is anxiety and puts you in a position to move forward.

A is for Adversity (or sometimes Activating event or Antecedent, i.e., what came before)

B is for Beliefs (that are triggered by the Adversity)

C is for Consequences (our behavioral and emotional response)

Very generally, if we can understand the events that trigger certain thoughts and beliefs, and how these then in turn create consequences for us (i.e., stress!), we can work backward to create a life that is closer to what we want.

Let's start with the activating event. This can be internal (for example, a headache) or external (for example, a comment from someone else). Now, these stimuli in themselves mean nothing. We come in with certain beliefs and interpretations about them, and these can be rational or irrational. Let's say you have a headache, and this activates certain (usually automatic) beliefs: *Just my luck. I'm not going to be able to do my work today. This is bad, and it's going to get worse . . . I can't believe this is happening to me.* These thoughts then trigger certain emotions, in this case fear and worry. Importantly, it's not the event itself, but our interpretation of it that creates anxiety.

But as you can see, the beliefs above are not exactly based in objective reality. They are distortions.

When we are stuck in anxious rumination, we think we are solving a problem by dwelling on our beliefs themselves; for example, we might think at length about how bad the headache is and how we are going to deal with the catastrophe it will turn out to be. But with the ABC model, what we do is examine the beliefs themselves. Who says the headache will be a catastrophe, anyway? We don't take for granted that our beliefs are always accurate!

If we feel anxious, it is usually because we hold beliefs, assumptions, and biases that trigger and maintain this anxiety. Change those beliefs and we remove the anxiety.

Here's another example. You find out that two of your friends are hanging out, but didn't invite you to join them (activating event). You think, "They've excluded me on purpose. Maybe they're talking about me right now" (beliefs), and as a result, you have trouble falling asleep that night, and the next morning, you are rude to both of them, causing upset (consequences).

Now, the ABC model helps us understand what has happened, but it also helps us go back and re-engineer situations so that we get the outcomes we want.

1. First, identify the **activating event**, trigger, or antecedent (not being invited)
2. Next, **identify how you feel** about this event or situation (ashamed, excluded, rejected)
3. Then, see if you can **find the belief** behind this response ("If they didn't invite me, it must be because they dislike me.")
4. Take a close look at this belief and ask whether it's really true. **Is it rational?** (The belief is not really rational since they could fail to invite you while still liking you. You realize that you have also spent time with them individually without inviting the other without intending any offense. You also realize that they are actually closer to one another than to you, and that this isn't the end of the world—other people can have close connections without it threatening you in any way!)
5. Try to recognize alternative interpretations of the situation, or **modify your belief** (Your friends have

not done anything *to* you. There isn't really a problem. In fact, seeing as they're doing a hobby you don't really like, you're a little relieved they didn't invite you . . .)

Everyone has different reactions to stress, and we may ourselves vary in our responses over time. But we can always become aware of and moderate these responses.

The ABC model helps us identify and change those irrational beliefs that cause anxiety. It's worth starting with emotions because they are usually at the forefront of our experience. If you feel angry, investigate whether a boundary or right has been violated. If you're sad, look at what has been potentially lost. Fear and anxiety can point to beliefs that dwell on threat—real or imagined. (Let's be honest, it's often imagined!) Guilt comes from the knowledge that we've violated someone's boundary.

Now, laying out examples on paper like this can make it seem fairly straightforward, but life is usually a bit more complicated. There are many ways we can use the ABC model. We can use it for small, individual scenarios as they unfold in the moment, or we can use it retroactively to dissect recurring overall themes and patterns in our lives. Or both!

When you're exploring antecedents, bear in mind that there could be many. It could be a person, an event, or just a situation. Consider the setting/environment, timing (the hour, day, time of year . . .), what sensory information is coming in, what *isn't* happening, people's behaviors or words, memories, (sometimes we don't even realize a memory has triggered us and instead think our anxiety has to do with what is happening in the present) or certain relationship dynamics.

Likewise, there may be many resulting beliefs and thoughts that are triggered. You may find that a surface level belief ("they've excluded me") sometimes conceals a deeper, more lasting core belief ("there is something wrong with who I am"). It's worth taking your time to dig a little.

Finally, consequences can be varied and play out on different time scales, too. We can ask what effects our beliefs have on us either in the short term or the long term. In our example, the short-term consequence is to lash out at the two friends, but in the longer term, you may discover that your core beliefs are actually getting in the way of your relationships in general.

How you use insights gained from the ABC model is up to you. But here are three questions that can help you reprogram your conditioned response from each level, A, B, or C:

A: Is it possible to change or remove certain triggers and antecedents? How?

B: If your resulting belief is irrational, how can you modify or completely replace it?

C: Can you change the consequences of your behaviors so that you reinforce the more rational beliefs?

If the ABC model doesn't quite work for you, take a look at the RAIN framework created by Michele McDonald, a renowned meditation teacher. It's simple:

RECOGNIZE/RELAX into what is emerging in your awareness (for example, your anxious feelings).
ACCEPT/ ALLOW it to simply be what it is.
INVESTIGATE the thoughts and emotions that emerge (this includes bodily sensations, too).
NOTE what is unfolding from one moment to the next.

Here's how that could look written as an inner self-dialogue: *So, I feel some stress coming on. I know this feeling. That's okay. I can let it happen, and it's not a problem. It really isn't. I'm going to relax and let this wave just pass. And it will pass. What is happening to me? I feel a weirdness in my chest. I recognize those core beliefs coming up in me, but I also notice that I'm not following that path into fear, either . . . I'm having an anxiety experience right now, and it's okay. In fact, I notice that it is already waning . . .*

The reason this RAIN technique works is because it puts us in a frame of mind that cannot co-exist with anxiety. When we are open, curious, and relaxed, we simply *can't* feel anxiety. So, what happens if we relax into our stress response and just become curious about it rather than fearing it and resisting it? Most of us know what it feels like to fear the fear. What does it feel like to be curious about it, instead?

Summary:

- Whatever form stress and anxiety take in your life, it's worth having some psychological tools to help you manage it mindfully. Build more self-awareness by learning to label your emotions and noting how they feel in your body in the moment. We can also build self-awareness by keeping a regular thought diary, or by taking psychometric tests.

- We don't have to accept our anxious thoughts as gospel. The Socratic questioning method asks us to look for evidence, become curious, and deliberately seek out alternative interpretations. We can likewise test our false beliefs by reappraising our assessment of the situation and the "threat" we see.

- Making a mind map gives us perspective and clarity on the chaos that may be in our minds. Start with a single word or phrase and do a "brain dump," then look for patterns and themes, asking what you can control and what you cannot. One of the best cures for anxiety is to ask what you can realistically **do** about your situation.

- The ABC model helps us understand the antecedents, beliefs, and consequences of our stress reaction, and allows us to re-engineer our perspective and behave differently.

- One option is to simply distract yourself by giving your brain an engaging "mind game."

Chapter 2. An Anxiety-Free Lifestyle

I don't have to tell you what a stressed-out lifestyle looks like, right? You're probably well aware of all the bad habits that accompany the stereotypical anxious day-to-day life: rushing, eating poorly, forgetting things, overworking, procrastinating, complaining, getting into arguments with others, biting your tongue, road rage, snapping at random people, falling asleep on the sofa, giving yourself a neck-ache because you've spent the day hunched and slouched over a laptop...

Your environment is actually an extension of your inner world. The everyday details of your life reflect your broader attitudes and values, and represent all the crystallized choices you've made in the past. In this way, the anxious mind can build a lifestyle and environment for itself that actually ends up creating more anxiety over time. For example, you are anxious and this makes you overwhelmed and disorganized, so you forget to pay a parking fine. The unpaid fine increases and, you guessed it, stresses you out even more, causing you to forget to do two more things... and the cycle continues.

In this chapter, we're looking at easy ways that you can start creating an environment that helps shape you in the opposite direction–that is, towards ease, confidence, relaxation and calm control. The idea is to structure your life in such a way that the easiest and most automatic response is always relaxation. In other words, you need to make an anxiety-free life your default.

8. LIMIT CAFFEINE INTAKE

Now, you might not want to hear what comes next, but if you're consistently battling anxiety, caffeine could be the hidden culprit. Did you know that the DSM—the *Diagnostic and Statistical Manual of Mental Disorders* used by the American Psychiatric Association—contains *four* separate disorders related to caffeine? Caffeine is the world's most commonly used psychoactive substance.

But Dr. Julie Radico is a clinical psychologist who reminds us that caffeine is not a problem per se—after all, it can boost concentration levels and give us a shot of energy. Not to mention it's delicious. "But I encourage people to know healthy limits and consume it strategically because it is activating and can mimic or exacerbate the symptoms of anxiety."

Because of the ubiquity of coffee in modern life, many of us (doctors included) simply never think of coffee as something that could be adding to our anxiety behind the scenes. So, we valiantly plug away at mindfulness and do our breathing exercises, conveniently forgetting the four cups of espresso we had that morning!

So, how much is too much? Well, there is variation in individual tolerance levels. The standard advice is not to exceed four hundred milligrams daily, or risk overstimulation, anxiety, and a range of fun physical effects such as nausea, gastrointestinal distress, and heart palpitations. For perspective, a normal cup of coffee brewed at home contains around one hundred milligrams of caffeine, but drinks sold in coffee shops and things like energy drinks or supplements can contain as much as four hundred milligrams in one cup. Cola can contain about thirty to fifty milligrams per can, and even tea and decaffeinated coffee can add to your overall caffeine intake, so don't assume that you're in the clear just because you don't drink coffee.

If you're a long-time coffee addict, you may not even know what your functioning is like without it. It's not an exaggeration to say that many people wrongly diagnose a caffeine-dependency as an anxiety disorder. These people have been dependent on caffeine for so long they simply assume the "wired-but-tired" feeling they experience day and night is just a part of their personality, or simply what life is like. If this sounds like you, then your next move is clear: build more awareness. First get a good idea of just exactly how much caffeine you're taking in on a daily and weekly basis-a diary or tracker will help. While we all differ in our ability to metabolize caffeine, you'll know that something is amiss if you can spot obvious links between your anxious feelings and your last cup. For example, if you tend to experience most anxiety, stress, and panic in the hour or two after drinking buckets of coffee, then the writing's on the wall.

So, is the solution to quit caffeine cold turkey? Probably not. Unless you are extremely sensitive to it or are battling a pronounced anxiety disorder, it's more about *moderation* and drinking coffee strategically than it is about quitting completely. A 2007 study by Sergi Ferré in the *Journal of Neurochemistry* explains exactly *why* coffee has the effects it does. Caffeine blocks the neurotransmitter adenosine, which results in us feeling more alert. But the same process also triggers adrenaline release. This process is not dissimilar from the one that unfolds in the HPA axis during the fight-or-flight response. Beyond a certain point, in other words, "alertness" turns into "anxiety."

A 2018 study by Winston et. al. in the journal *Advances in Psychiatric Treatment* found that a too-high caffeine intake can actually mimic the symptoms of a range of psychiatric disorders—including anxiety. This is important: it means that there are at least some people out there who have been diagnosed with an anxiety disorder, when the real story is that they are suffering from excessive caffeine intake. We can also infer that if you do have an intrinsic anxiety disorder, you may be turbo-charging it by throwing caffeine at the problem.

If this sounds like your situation, then the way forward may entail quitting or drastically reducing the amount of caffeine you take in.

Trying to stop abruptly may lead to caffeine withdrawal, which can be counterproductive. Instead, taper off gradually, find a comfortable dose that's right for you, and don't exceed it.

There are plenty of caffeine substitutes and beverages containing lower amounts of caffeine that you can use to gradually reduce your intake. Consider trying:

- **Matcha and green tea** – both very healthy and will also supply slow-release energy and focus
- **Black teas and herbal teas** contain smaller amounts of caffeine so you'll get a more moderate boost while staying hydrated
- **Chicory coffee and dandelion coffee** taste similar to regular coffee and are much healthier
- Finally, it may not seem very exciting, but try **plain water** – often, our feelings of fatigue come down to simple dehydration, and a glass of water may perk you up more than another cup of coffee. Add a little cucumber or lemon to make it fancy.

1. SCHEDULE YOUR "WORRY TIME"

Stress is a part of life. And we've already briefly explored the power of acceptance and acknowledgement without resistance. If worrying has been a constant part of your life that it almost seems like a day job, maybe it's time to turn things around and be the boss. How? One counterintuitive way is to deliberately dedicate time in your schedule to worry. In other words, give yourself permission to worry, but do it on your own terms.

If you're used to thinking of your anxiety as some annoying, difficult, or even shameful tendency, then it might feel strange at first to "worry more effectively." But let's start with an assumption: you will probably worry at least somewhat some of the time. So, choose *how* you do it. Here's a suggestion:

Step 1: Be aware of when you're worrying.
Step 2: Acknowledge that you're "allowed" to feel worried—but that you'll merely delay worrying for later.
Step 3: Pick up your worry again later at some pre-planned, limited time window in the future.

That's all there is to it. It may feel counterintuitive, but once you try it, you may feel a kind of paradoxical relief. Sometimes, a weird thing can happen with anxiety. It's a little like the thing that happens when people announce that they're going on a diet and giving up chocolate. Suddenly, the only thing they want in the world is chocolate. Chocolate becomes the madly desirable thing. You get the idea. By forbidding it, the thing becomes instantly more attractive, and cheating is framed as a kind of treat.

Worry is similar. You are trying to stop worry, but not because worry is some special, forbidden thing. This way, the worry itself has no hold on you either way.

You cannot do this process if you're not first mindful of what's happening. Don't be too hard on yourself if you slip into unconscious rumination now and again—practice makes perfect. Simply be glad when you "come back" to awareness and carry on without beating yourself up for getting trapped in a loop.

Next, say to the worry, "I see you. I'll give you all the attention you need, but not right now." Then, perhaps jot down some notes to help remind you later. Have a "worry book"—once a thought is in there, it's safe and you don't need to return to it until the designated worry time. Your mind will want to return there, but politely remind it, "You don't have to do anything right now, mind. Nothing is outstanding, and there is no problem to solve right now. For the time being, we only have to relax. You can worry as much as you like . . . later."

If you are having particular trouble with delaying worries, simply write *that* worry down in the book, too! For example, "I'm really worried that this stupid technique is actually going to ruin my life." Your brain will play a trick on you. It will try to argue that worrying is a useful thing, and that by not worrying, you're doing something wrong or allowing everything to go haywire. Just notice this and give yourself permission to put all that rumination aside for the time being. You can catastrophize later as much as you want!

Okay, so when do you actually worry?

Allocate a time (around twenty minutes) once a day when there are no restrictions, and you can worry to your heart's content. In fact, during this time, you're not allowed to do anything other than go through your worry book and worry. Completely focus on your worries. Note how it feels to worry now after a day spent not worrying. You may notice a few unexpected things:

- The thoughts you believed were really, really important a few hours ago don't quite seem as urgent now
- We are capable of "sitting with" anxiety
- Our worrying doesn't actually change anything—because we can stop doing it and life just carries on as it did before
- Worrying actually doesn't feel very good (this sounds obvious, but it can be a lightbulb moment for some people— why spend so much time deliberately making yourself feel bad—especially when it doesn't achieve a single thing?)

The next time an "urgent" worry comes up, you might find yourself wondering, "How is this going to look to me a few hours from now? Is it really as urgent as it feels?"

Sometimes, you'll look at a thought you've written down and be comfortable completely crossing it off the list. It's no longer relevant, so congratulations, you spared yourself some unnecessary worry! But sometimes you'll put something in your worry book that *is* genuinely a problem. Then what? As before, we need to become aware of what we can control, what we can't, what we value, and what action we can take. Worry can serve a purpose—it can alert us to problems and inspire us to solve them by taking action.

There is an Erma Bombeck quote: "Worrying is like a rocking chair. It will give you something to do, but it won't get you anywhere." Instead of just going back and forth, commit to busting worries by *doing* something about them.

Your scheduled worry time can be used to simply worry, but you can also take it a step further. Look at everything you've written down and categorize it. What is in your control and actionable? What isn't? What is you trying to people-please or solve problems that are not your business to solve? Can you see any items that are just mindless what-if questions, regrets, or distorted beliefs?

Once you've had a look at the actual content of your worrying mind, it's a great idea to take one simple next step: look at all the problems you can actually do something about and identify only the very next small step you need to take to get started.

For example, if you've been worrying about how you're going to manage catering for a massive party at the end of the week, your very next action might be to confirm the actual guest numbers so you know how many you're catering for. Don't think beyond this, just identify this next step and then take it. Often, your very next step will simply be planning some time in your schedule for when you'll work on the issue at hand. Once you've scheduled blocks of time this way, put the issue out of your mind. If you're someone who gets worried about forgetting things, then set a reminder that will work for you and then forget about it.

This "forgetting about it" is where the real work takes place. You'll gradually learn to trust yourself. If you've done what you can, you can rest. Eventually, with practice and with using the above techniques, you will actually prove to yourself that your worry is kind of useless, and that you can manage your life perfectly well without it!

Think of it as developing an attitude of healthy boundaries. Imagine your worry is like a pushy relative who never shuts up and never leaves you alone. You need to learn to say no to them! You also need to learn to tell yourself that worrying is not the same as problem solving. **Do** something to solve the problem, and if you can't, then it's not worth worrying about, right? Scheduling worry teaches you an important lesson: that *you* are in control of your thoughts. They are not in control of you.

2. CULTIVATE GRATITUDE

By now, there is so much evidence for the value of being thankful for the positive things in our lives that you'll see gratitude practice suggested as a solution for just about anything. But did you know that being grateful can also help you lower stress levels? It's easy to understand why. When you're anxious and overthinking, your brain is hyper aware of everything that's wrong, exaggerating perceived threats and dwelling on all the bad things that could potentially happen. But when you are grateful, your brain does the opposite—it zooms in on what's important, what's right, and what's going well.

Remember the hand that is held right in front of your face, so that you can't see or think about anything else around you? Anxiety is not a million miles away from ingratitude. It is our ability to hyper-focus on the tiny dust bunny in the corner of the room, and ignore how wonderfully clean and tidy the rest of the room is. It is our ability to allow a tiny problem (a single, ambiguous comment received from a friend) to completely eclipse the many wonderful things also happening (the dozens of obvious compliments you also received).

Being grateful is not just a box we tick or something we do once and never again. It's a habit. It's an attitude. It's also an entire perspective and orientation to life itself. A 2008 longitudinal study by Wood et. al. published in the *Journal of Research in Personality* found that gratitude improved relationships, strengthened mental resilience, and lowered anxiety. When we are grateful, we are:

- Less self-critical and easier on ourselves
- More compassionate with others
- More relaxed and able to enjoy our good fortune
- More creative, curious and exploratory
- Able to give support and seek it from others
- More aware of opportunities, options, and solutions
- Better equipped to bounce back from adversity
- More trusting of the general goodwill of the world around us

Being grateful doesn't mean we don't experience adversity and disappointment. It just means we deal with these things more easily. Why? Because those negative experiences never dominate or define your entire life, but rather they are seen against a rich backdrop of many other things in your world, some of which are going pretty well.

A 2019 German study by Heckendorf et. al. (*Behavior Research and Therapy*) discovered a significant reduction in anxious negative self-talk when study participants used an app that helped them cultivate more gratitude day to day. It's this ability to think differently about adversity that helps us stress less about it.

You might be tempted to think of keeping a gratitude journal as a kind of trendy fad that couldn't possibly help combat all the genuinely terrifying things in your life. But practicing gratitude can literally change your brain. Anxiety can cause us to release stress hormones and neurotransmitters that teach us to look for the negative in our lives. And when we look, we can usually find something to worry about! And the cycle continues.

Isn't it a mind-blowing idea–the nature of your perception and the things you choose to place your attention on can literally influence your physical makeup. If we are anxious and ungrateful, we take the worst parts of life, amplify them, zoom in on them, and make them the be-all-and-end-all. But if we're grateful, we create a neurochemical environment that primes us to see the good instead. And the more good we see, the better we are at seeing it.

You cannot be grateful and anxious at the same time. I dare you to try it!

If we choose gratitude, it displaces stress. After all, stress is not just a response—it's a perspective and an attitude. And attitudes can change. You can choose to focus on the thought, "Look how blessed I am!" instead of, "Look how much is wrong with everything." You don't literally change reality, but you do choose which parts to take in, to focus on, and to make bigger.

Sounds good, but how do you actually practice gratitude and switch away from anxiety (an ungrateful state)? First of all, don't fake it! Going through the motions will get you nowhere. The first step is just to become aware. Human beings tend to enjoy the good things in their lives at first, but quickly become numb to them over time, taking them for granted precisely because those good things are so abundant.

Instead, consciously look around your life and really see all the great things you have. Find beauty around you. Even if you're having a hard time with the rose-tinted glasses, pause and appreciate the fact that you are a completely unique human being who is doing their best to be their best. Isn't that wonderful in itself? That you're trying?

What have you achieved that you're not giving yourself full credit for?

What is working well for you right now?

In what ways have you been given perks, privileges and lucky breaks that you didn't strictly deserve?

Who has helped you or supported you, even when they could have easily not done so?

In what ways are the people around you actually quite awesome?

What could have gone wrong, but actually didn't?

Can you see how your life has a lot of good in it, even though there are always problems, too?

The conventional advice is to "write five things in a notebook you're grateful for every day," and this is great advice. But gratitude is not just singling out this and that, rather, it's a complete mindset switch. When you adopt this frame of mind, everything looks different. It's not that you are tasked with thinking of the nice things in your life—it's that you change your attitude in such a way that *everything* in your life looks a little nicer than it did before. You know—the opposite of what anxiety does!

Gratitude takes practice. It takes time to shift your mindset, but it can be done. Author of *Emotional First Aid* Dr. Guy Winch claims that gratitude acts like a kind of mental immunization against stress. When we are grateful, we flood our brains with calm-inducing serotonin and dopamine. We feel happier and more at ease. We are better able to tolerate uncertainty. "Gratitude is an emotion that grounds us and is a great way to balance out the negative mindset that uncertainty engenders," he says.

Gratitude is a daily habit as important as eating right and exercising. And it all comes down to *focus*—i.e., where we choose to put our attention. Have you ever noticed if someone you know is pregnant, suddenly all you seem to see around you are pregnant women? It's the same with gratitude. When you deliberately put your attention on the good, you will suddenly seem to find it all over the place.

Gratitude Tip 1

Wake up every morning and, first thing, pause and reflect on everything you have to be grateful for. Take stock of your blessings. What are you learning every day? What opportunities are there? What have you taken for granted? What beautiful things surround you? What is better today than it was a year ago? What has someone done for you that you're happy about?

Dwelling on the answers to these questions will help you set your emotional tone for the day. You don't need to do anything special, just pause and deliberately appreciate how great some things actually are. Do it every morning before you even step out of bed.

Gratitude Tip 2

Keep a journal. First thing in the morning or last thing at night, use journaling to reflect on the day and what went well with it. Really dwell on the positive emotions. Write a love letter to your life telling it how glad you are that it is what it is! Try not to mechanically write the same things over and over again. The exercise is about more than making a list. You want to give your brain time to genuinely experience all those happy neurotransmitters!

Even if you're having a hard time, try to focus on the positive within that. You've come down with the flu? Well, at least you have someone to take care of you, and time to catch up on some trashy reality TV! You got some bad feedback for a work project? But thinking about it, hasn't your critic also kind of done you a favor by drawing your attention to what can be improved? Looking for the silver lining sounds cheesy, but there almost always is one.

Gratitude Tip 3

Don't just keep all those warm, fuzzy feelings to yourself, though. Whenever you can remember, ask if there's someone in your world who you could show a little more appreciation to. Demonstrating how thankful we are for other people not only makes us feel amazing, it'll do the same for them!

Too often we don't say just how much we love and appreciate those around us. Why keep it a secret? Think of someone you haven't spoken to in a while, but who you'd be devastated to never hear from again. Reach out to them and be earnest and complimentary. Write a sincere thank you note to someone who's made a difference in your life. Give gifts, leave little encouraging notes for others to find, or simply make a point of telling the barista at the coffee shop that they've made your day with their incredible mocha.

Gratitude Tip 4

Practice a bit of "reverse complaining." Chronic low-grade complaining is a deadly habit that many of us get trapped in without realizing. We may believe that we are simply making neutral observations, or that we are merely perfectionists with high standards, but complaining is like drinking one tiny drop of poison after another.

When you notice yourself griping and whining about things, actively notice what's happening and deliberately counter it with a bit of "reverse complaining" which is nothing more than choosing to practice gratitude instead. As though you were switching cameras, choose to focus on something else entirely. You could complain about the rain, but why not be thankful instead that your garden is getting a good drink of water?

You could notice the urge to start moaning internally about your friend's lateness meeting you at the cafe, but choose to pull out your phone and enjoy a few happy moments reading instead. Your friend is going to be late one way or another, but you are the one who chooses whether to be annoyed by that or not.

3. USE "MENTAL ANCHORING"

If anxiety, rumination, and overthinking are like powerful overwhelming waves, then "mental anchoring" is a way to grab hold of something and stay stable in the flood. Mental anchoring is a popular technique used to manage panic attacks, but can help any time we need to ground ourselves.

It works because of the brain's tendency to create links and associations. The technique is based in NLP, or Neurolinguistic Programming, and allows us to grab hold of a kind of primary experience and create a path back to it so we can access it later when we need it—i.e., in moments of anxiety or panic.

Michael Carroll is the founder of the NLP Academy and teaches people the simple four-step process: first, you access a particular state, then you find an anchoring stimulus in that state, and then you exit that state. When you're done, you can test the anchor if you like.

Before we explain what this means, let's consider the type of anchors you can have—all are based in our sensory perception:

Visual anchors: something you can see internally (like the image of a peaceful beach) or externally (like a red string tied round your wrist).

Auditory anchors: something you can hear internally (repeating to yourself a mantra) or externally (ringing a bell, whistling, or clicking your fingers).

Kinesthetic anchors: something to do with touch or movement (such as drawing a shape on the back of your hand or pressing the soft spot of flesh between index finger and thumb).

Olfactory anchors: something you can smell (for example, a little spritz bottle of lavender essential oil).

Gustatory anchors: something you can taste (for example, mint chewing gum).

Now, let's say you were feeling anxious and wanted to feel calmer and in control. You would think back to a moment in the past when you felt how you'd like to feel now. For example, you might choose a peaceful memory you have of camping with your family in the forest. Take your time sinking into this memory, reliving it on all the sensory channels you can—dwell on what you smell, see, touch, etc.

As you relive this memory, you start to relive the feelings of calm and control you felt then. Really dig deep into these feelings and how they connect to your sensory memories. See the beautiful green trees swaying around you, smell the fresh air, feel the warmth of the sun on your skin. When you are at the "peak" of this emotional state, quickly connect it to your chosen anchor. For example, you might rub your fingers over a smooth polished quartz stone you can keep in your pocket. This quartz stone now becomes an anchor back into this peaceful moment. The anchor does not have to relate to the memory for the association to work.

You can test to see if this association has cemented itself by later running your fingers over the smooth stone in some other context. Are you immediately reminded of the forest and the sun again? Bear in mind that making the link may take a few attempts. Anchoring is essentially reprogramming your brain. For it to work best, be consistent and keep repeating the stimulus with the anchor to tie them together. Remember to pair the anchor to the *peak* of your emotional experience. This takes a little practice, so be patient.

Later in this book, we'll explore other ways to use our senses to anchor in the present moment and cut anxiety as it's happening. But for now, the NLP mental anchoring technique is a great way to prepare yourself ahead of time to better manage overwhelming feelings as they emerge.

The great thing about anchoring is that your body and mind are already doing it. After all, your anxiety response might be nothing more than a series of negative associations you've made. For example, you might catch a whiff of the scent your awful ex used to wear and suddenly be reminded of all the negative feelings you have around that breakup. Or you could hear certain words or phrases that remind you of painful, traumatic, or just embarrassing moments from your past—like a magic spell, it almost seems to transport you right back into that state of mind!

With this technique, you are taking your brain's propensity to make associations and using it for good. The technique can be used to break certain associations *and* make new ones. There is no limit to the kind or number of associations you make—all you need to do is be aware of the rules your brain follows to make those associations and consciously choose to make them in a way that helps you live the life you want to live.

It is as though we take a "button"—i.e., a stimulus or anchor—and wire it up to a desired mental state; for example, calmness. We want to connect our brains in such a way that when we push the button, we feel the state of mind we want to feel.

Here's a summary of the steps you need to follow to do this wiring-up process. It's not enough to simply read about them and intellectually grasp the idea—you need to try these steps for yourself and literally *experience* the associations in your own brain. The experience is what strengthens the connection.

Step 1: Choose a desired state of mind.

Step 2: Choose an anchor.

Step 3: Explore in full detail a memory where you felt the desired state.

Step 4: At the emotional peak of the memory, capture the feeling with your anchor.

Step 5: Repeat—as many as five or ten times—to cement the association.

Step 6: Test the connection by engaging the anchor and noticing whether you conjure the desired emotion.

Step 7: If it doesn't work, drill the association a few more times, or pick a stronger memory to work with.

4. HAVE A SOLID MORNING ROUTINE

Anxiety and overthinking are about the individual distorted thoughts we have and the anxious actions we choose in one moment or another. But anxiety is also an overall attitude that colors everything in life like a filter. That attitude cannot help but manifest itself externally in the form of our daily habits and actions. To tackle anxiety, we need to work on multiple levels at once–we need to address distorted thoughts and feelings, but also consider how those thoughts and feelings are rippling out into our everyday lives. Changing one will lead to changes in the other. Very simply, changing your mind will lead to lifestyle changes, but the relationship goes the other way, too; changing your lifestyle will also impact your thoughts and feelings.

We need consistent daily habits, routines, and ways of seeing that cultivate feelings of calm, relaxation, and control. This is why a morning routine is so important. A good morning routine sets the pattern for the rest of the day. Your ideal stress-busting routine will not be exactly the same as everyone else's, but it turns out that there are a few scientifically proven activities that will definitely boost your mood and ward off anxiety. How you include some of these ideas is up to you.

Drink water

Amanda Carlson is a registered dietician and director of nutrition at Athletes' Performance, which is responsible for training world-class athletes. "Studies have shown that being just half a liter dehydrated can increase your cortisol levels," she says. And more cortisol means more stressed feelings. "When you don't give your body the fluids it needs, you're putting stress on it, and it's going to respond to that." But being stressed itself can also lead to dehydration . . . which can make you more stressed, creating a vicious cycle.

One simple way to fend off dehydration is to always keep a glass of water next to your bed. Drink water first thing in the morning.

Enjoy nature

You don't need to go outside into the woods for a walk first thing in the morning. (Although if you can, great!) But do take some time to enjoy the natural, non-manmade world to ground yourself in the morning. This could be:

- Opening your window the moment you wake up to take deep breaths of fresh morning air.
- Having your breakfast in your garden, maybe even putting bare feet in the grass.
- Play some soothing nature sounds (oceans, birdsong, rainstorms, etc.) as you get ready for the day, or enjoy a few YouTube videos of relaxing nature scenes, cute cats, or beautiful scenery.

- Really enjoy something wholesome and natural to eat, like some fresh fruit.
- Get outside in the sunshine, smell the rain, or take a moment to enjoy the birds on your windowsill.

Eat well

According to the National Institute of Mental Health (NIMH), chronic stress can increase your risk for developing obesity, heart disease, depression, type 2 diabetes, and anxiety. Everyday Health ran a survey in 2019 of 6,700 Americans, where thirty-five percent rated their stress levels as a six or a seven on a scale from one to seven. And that was before the pandemic! The most common way of dealing with stress? Food. And you can guess that the foods chosen were not fruit smoothies and broccoli.

Ali Miller is a dietician and author of *The Anti-Anxiety Diet* and claims that the key to a stress-busting diet is to maintain stable blood sugar levels. This means avoiding refined carbs that can spike blood sugar and insulin levels, then crash, exacerbating stress on the body. Instead, choose high-fiber foods and whole grains, and avoid fasting or binging. Likewise, healthy fats slow digestion and increase satiety, so eat things like eggs, avocados, and nuts to help balance stress hormones and regulate your mood.

Commit to having a light, wholesome breakfast every morning: for example, some oatmeal with raisins and cinnamon, a mushroom and spinach omelet, or some whole grain toast with peanut butter. Choose foods that make you happy, like a single block of dark chocolate (yes, a 2009 study by Martin et. al. in the *Journal of Proteome Research* found that modest daily chocolate intake lowered stress hormone levels). Have some coffee-but not too much-or try tea. A 2013 study in the *Journal of Psychopharmacology* discovered that chamomile actually alters the body's stress response and stimulates the release of feel-good neurotransmitters.

One tip is to add a banana to your breakfast. A preliminary study in *Neuropharmacology* found that depression and anxiety could be a result of magnesium deficiency. Bananas are rich in magnesium, not to mention potassium and B vitamins, which regulate the nervous system and ease fatigue. Other foods to include are oily fish (rich in brain healthy Omega 3), milk (calcium deficiency has been associated with poor mood), and fruit (vitamin C may lower cortisol levels).

Avoid too much caffeine, refined sugar, and alcohol, and don't allow yourself to get too hungry, nor to have meals that are too big and heavy. Eat mindfully, go easy on yourself when you're not perfect, and remember that food is a source of joy and wellbeing.

The best way to get a solid morning routine going is to be realistic and start small. Don't try to completely makeover your life in twenty-four hours. If you make it enjoyable, you're more likely to stick to it, so choose small changes that will actually work for your lifestyle and the kind of person you are. For example, if you hate cooking and have a tiny kitchen and a busy job, don't go and buy a giant smoothie maker and force yourself to concoct elaborate breakfast smoothies in the morning—you'll only increase stress, not lower it!

Be consistent and patient. Know that slipping up here and there is not the end of the world. Be flexible so that if something isn't really working, you don't have to completely give up—just become curious about what *will* work. Always remember that self-care is about loving your body and enjoying life; it shouldn't feel like hard work or a punishment!

Here are a few more things you can build into your morning routine, but again, don't feel pressured to do all of them. Sometimes, the small changes make the biggest difference if they are changes that fit, that are chosen mindfully, and that are done consistently.

- Don't look at your phone first thing in the morning. Keep it in another room.
- Meditate, read a few pages from an inspirational book, pray, or do a contemplative exercise.
- Take a few deep breaths.
- Spend some quality time with loved ones or even with pets.
- Stretch or do some quick yoga.
- Do a visualization for the day ahead, or say some affirmations.
- Indulge in a self-care treat like a special bath, some lovely music, or a delicious snack you reserve for mornings only.
- Take care with a dressing, grooming, and getting-ready ritual that helps you feel cared for.
- Drink water, tea, or coffee, and really savor it along with your healthy breakfast. Don't eat while distracted.
- Be mindful with everything you do. Get up early so you can take your time. Feel the bubbles of your shampoo in your hair. Dress with care. Enjoy the quiet, private ritual of drinking some tea, sitting down with a gratitude journal, or making some goals for the day ahead.

A morning routine, whatever it looks like, does one important thing: it tells your body and mind that whatever happens, you're in calm control. You're the boss. You set your intention, and you follow through. Every day.

5. START A HOBBY

A 2013 study in the *Mental Health Review Journal* found that "gardening-based interventions for people experiencing mental health difficulties reported that benefits include a reduction in symptoms of depression and anxiety and an increase in attentional capacity and self-esteem. Key benefits include emotional benefits such as reduced stress and improved mood." A *Frontiers in Psychology* paper published in 2021 also found that people who indulged in their cooking hobby during the Covid-19 lockdowns experienced stress reduction and better resilience.

So, does this mean we have to take up gardening or baking to beat our stress? Nope! It may simply be that hobbies—whatever they are—can improve our overall wellbeing and make us more resilient to everyday stress. Having a pastime is a great way to ease your mind and just focus on something else. A hobby can also give you a sense of pride when a goal is accomplished, and if it's a social hobby, you get all the benefits of friendly interaction with others.

If you have a project that you've been putting off, it might be time to pick it up again. But if you're in the market for a new hobby, the golden rule when it comes to hobbies is that they should be fun! If you're not really enjoying something, give yourself full permission to drop it. If cooking and gardening seem like torture to you, don't force yourself. Sometimes, those of us with tendencies toward anxiety can put a lot of pressure on ourselves to do things "right" or get hung up on the outcome rather than just enjoying the process as it unfolds.

You'll know a hobby is the right one for you when you feel pleasantly distracted and look forward to picking it up again. You should feel refreshed and relaxed by it rather than seeing it as another thing on the to-do list. Here are a few things to try:

Arts and crafts: Try your hand at drawing and painting, compiling scrap books, collage making, knitting and crochet, sewing clothing and quilt making, woodwork, metalwork, mosaics, making candles or soap, flower arranging, jewelry making, interior design, or leatherwork.

Music: Either listening to it or making it. Join a choir or sign up for drumming lessons, or just tinker with your ultimate playlist. You can do official classes with a teacher or just get a simple instrument to play around with.

Writing: Write stories, poems, novels, letters, articles, or keep a journal. Think about joining a writing group or a flash poetry club. Why not enter competitions?

Physical activity: Exercising, dancing, swimming, hiking, walking, surfing, martial arts, extreme sports, spending time with animals, camping, or gymnastics are all great options.

Reading: There's a whole world of things to read! Subscribe to a new magazine, try a classic novel, consider joining a reading club, or go to talks by famous authors.

Socializing: Join a Meetup group where you can chat and connect with people of all kinds, spend time with family, join a book club or support group, or start a group of your own.

Everything else: Cooking, gardening, photography, wild foraging, pottery, calligraphy, building puzzles or miniature models, flying kites, decorating cakes, keeping chickens, baskets and weaving, car restoration, dog and cat breeding, standup comedy or improv, collecting comic books, horse-riding, rock-collecting, glass-blowing, hang-gliding, or joining an amateur drama group might be the hobby you're looking for.

Be honest about which hobbies genuinely make you feel good, which ones are a good fit for you personally, and which ones are likely to make you feel happier and more relaxed. Sometimes, we can get caught up in a hobby because we're very competitive, or feel like we should do it because we have some talent in that area, or simply because it's what others expect of us. Maybe we feel that we need to have hobbies for others to find us interesting. Drop all of these assumptions and choose something that genuinely makes you feel good. If your ideal hobby is buying air-dry clay from the craft store and making random misshapen animals for a few hours on the weekend, then do that!

Try to choose hobbies that have other benefits, too. For example, joining a gym and doing Pilates is a hobby that may make you feel good, but it also improves your physical fitness and floods your body with endorphins, building long-term stress resilience. So, you benefit from *two* forms of anxiety management. Or you could volunteer at an animal shelter because you love cats, but get the additional feel-good benefits from knowing you've helped animals in need. And by learning to cook better, you de-stress, improve your nutrition, and do something for your family that bolsters your relationship with them. All of this indirectly improves wellbeing and reduces stress.

As with all other routines, start small and be consistent. It's better to experiment a little at first to see if you like something, then ramp it up as you go. The only rule is that you enjoy yourself! Avoid spending too much money on equipment at first, and don't get too hung up if you skip a few lessons or don't do especially well in the beginning. The goal is not to become a virtuoso, but to have some fun. So, if you've given it a good shot and find that you're not getting much from a new hobby, don't worry about quitting and looking for something you like better.

Summary:

- Easy, everyday lifestyle changes can make a big difference with anxiety and overthinking. An obvious area to examine is whether you're having too much caffeine. Try to limit yourself to four hundred milligrams daily.

- Everyone worries, so at least do it strategically by scheduling worry time. Keep a worry journal so that instead of fighting worry, you postpone and contain it, tackling it on your own terms.
- Practice gratitude daily to gently shift your perspective to focus on everything that is going well in your world. Use a journal or write thank-you notes to people who have shown you kindness.
- Mental anchoring is a technique that, once established, can be used as often as you like to help ground and calm you. Choose an anchor, choose a desired state, then connect the two during visualization so that revisiting the anchor brings you back to that state of mind.
- Have a consistent morning routine where you focus on good food, nature, healthy habits, and quiet contemplative time where you set your intention for the day. Make sure you're hydrated, since dehydration can elevate cortisol levels.
- Finally, choose a hobby that can act as a pleasant distraction—but make sure you're choosing something you genuinely enjoy.

Chapter 3. Enter Your Mind

No book on stress management and anxiety reduction would be complete without a section on meditation and mindfulness. In fact, meditation is rightly considered one of the best and most effective ways to regulate your stress response and access a more tranquil and controlled state of mind.

However, don't worry if you have never really enjoyed formal meditation or feel like you may lack the time or wherewithal. The mindfulness techniques discussed in this chapter are easy and accessible and can be done anywhere, anytime, with very little practice. The great thing about them is how easily they can be combined with the other strategies covered in this book!

6. BELLY BREATHING

One excellent technique to start with is a deceptively simple one: belly breathing, also known as diaphragmatic breathing. Instead of breathing from the chest, belly breathing is about deeper, fuller breaths that originate from the diaphragm, which is a large dome-shaped muscle in your abdomen. When you breathe in, the diaphragm tightens and moves down, creating more space in your lungs that draws air in. When you exhale, the diaphragm relaxes, and this contracts the lungs, expelling air out.

This type of breathing encourages full oxygen exchange, which in turn slows the heartbeat and lowers blood pressure. All of this spells more relaxation of your entire body, less physiological arousal, and a more balanced stress response.

The next time you're feeling ultra-stressed, pause and notice what your breath is doing. Often, we breathe incorrectly without even knowing we're doing it. Anxious breathing tends to be shallow and rapid—it's part of our fight-or-flight response. Even though we were all born with the knowledge of how to breathe deeply (watch how a baby breathes!) we can learn bad habits as we grow up and favor smaller, tighter chest breathing. But if we relearn this skill, we give ourselves a tool to quickly relax our bodies via our breath.

By slowing our breath, we slow our thoughts and bring ourselves into a more relaxed frame of mind.

So how do you do belly breathing? Thankfully, it's something anyone can learn to do, and it can be done anywhere, anytime.

1. Find a comfortable spot to sit or lie down, checking to see that you're not slouching or holding tension in your muscles.
2. Close your eyes or, if you're more practiced, keep them softly gazing in the middle distance.
3. Put one hand on your belly and the other on your chest.
4. Breathe normally and notice the movement of your hands with your body. Try to breathe deeply so that the hand on your belly is moving up and down more than the hand on your chest.
5. Take more deep breaths, focusing on keeping the breath in your belly.

Breathe in through your nose and imagine you're blowing yourself up like a balloon. Exhale slowly through the mouth, almost like you're whistling, but without sound.

And that's it! When we are deeply relaxed, we tend to breathe like this anyway. But if we can pause during stressful moments and train ourselves to breathe like this on purpose, we encourage ourselves to relax and slow down. Shallow chest breathing is unfortunately the norm, but it is associated with tension, both muscular and psychological. Just practice shallow, quick breathing at the "top of your lungs" for a minute or so and then notice what emotions you feel afterward!

Belly breathing is a wonderful thing to do first thing in the morning, almost as though you are waking your lungs up and filling every cell in your body with fresh clean air. As you breathe, you could even use visualization to imagine that you're exhaling stress and worry and inhaling peace, calm, and happiness (we'll look at visualization techniques in more detail later on).

A few things to avoid:

- Belly breathing is not about *forcing* anything, either the inhale or the exhale.
- Sometimes, when people relax some parts of their body, they inadvertently tighten and tense other parts. Be aware of your entire body and try to gently release any tension that you notice–again, not forcing, but simply *releasing*.
- If you're in an active anxiety spiral or are feeling panicky, try to relax first before attempting belly breathing.

A 2017 paper published in *Frontiers in Psychology* by Xiao Ma and colleagues found that belly breathing triggers the body's natural relaxation response, which then has positive benefits on the psychological experience of stress. The researchers took forty participants and randomly assigned them either to a control group or a group that completed a belly breathing intervention. This intervention included twenty intensive breathing training sessions over eight weeks. These participants learned to breathe at an average rate of around four breaths per minute.

All forty participants completed tests for attention, mood, and cortisol levels, both before the eight-week period and after. The results showed that the intervention group had better moods, better attention, and lower salivary cortisol levels, suggesting they were less stressed overall. If these participants could achieve all that in just eight weeks, what could you do if you had the rest of your life to master deep belly breathing?

Now, as with all mindfulness techniques, not every approach is going to work for everyone. For some, focusing so closely on the breath can actually exacerbate anxious feelings. One thing to bear in mind is that when we are extremely relaxed and calm, our breathing can sometimes become more shallow. When we are sleeping, for example, our breath is very light, shallow, and regular. In this case, pushing yourself to do deep belly breaths may feel *less* relaxing, not more.

If you do notice yourself feeling awkward, panting, holding your breath, or getting worried about whether you're doing it right, pause and come back to the exercise later. It doesn't mean that breathing exercises are not right for you, and it certainly doesn't mean you're doing anything wrong; it just means that something else might work better. Yoga breathing, or the 5-4-3-2-1 grounding technique (discussed in the next section) may work better for you.

You could also use an app to help guide your breathing practice, or even seek out the help of a therapist. It may work for you to pair breathing exercises with another relaxation technique like guided imagery, chanting, or singing, or something like Tai Chi. That said, it's worth noting that diaphragmatic breathing may feel strange at first, so don't worry if it takes a little while to become familiar with it.

1. THE 5-4-3-2-1 GROUNDING TECHNIQUE

Anxiety has a funny way of fueling itself. We can get caught in loops, and a negative thought or sensation, when focused on, seems to grow larger and larger . . . and soon we're panicking about how much we're panicking. This is in effect what happens in a panic attack. Isn't it strange how a person can be in the grips of the most terrifying experience of their lives, convinced they're about to die, even though they're *in reality* just sitting in a mall where nothing is going on and they're perfectly safe? Such is the power of the mind!

Grounding techniques work because they recognize that anxiety is about detaching our senses from the real world. Ordinarily, our fight-or-flight response is there to keep us safe from real dangers in the present moment. But with anxiety, the danger is only imagined. We respond to something that actually isn't happening to us.

There is one sure-fire way to come out of this mental loop: get back into our bodies. The mind can carry us to the past to stress about things that have already happened, or to the future to things that haven't happened yet (and may never happen), but when we stay in the *present*, we notice how little there is to actually fear right in front of us. Your brain can rush around in a million directions, but your body can only ever be in one place—the present. Connect to that present by anchoring in your body's senses.

Here's how to do the 5-4-3-2-1 grounding technique. Unlike some techniques, it's quite easy to remember, and you can mix it up a little without changing the overall effectiveness. Try it any time you're feeling stressed and overwhelmed, or when your mind is getting caught up in a reinforcing loop. It's effective for moments of overthinking and overwhelm, can be used after a big upset, or if you're feeling yourself slip into a panic attack. You only need a few minutes.

First, just take a few deep breaths and orient yourself. Then:

Find FIVE things around you that you can SEE. Completely immerse yourself in the sense of sight. Find something in your environment and focus on it. Its precise texture, its color, its shape—just explore the object with your eyes. Do this for four more things.

Then, find FOUR things that you can TOUCH. Maybe you notice the feeling of the fabric on the chair you're sitting on, or the feeling of your hair against your cheek.

Next, find THREE things that you can HEAR. There's no need to identify positive or negative, good or bad. Just listen. You might hear the low hum of a computer, birds outside, or chatting next door.

Then, find TWO things you can SMELL. Some people can find this difficult, but if you pay attention, you may notice there are actually plenty of smells all around you!

Finally, find ONE thing that you can TASTE. This may simply be the lingering taste of coffee on your tongue, or you may detect a faint taste of toothpaste. If you can and you want to, nibble on something nearby or take a sip of something, even if it's just water.

What's the point of all of this? Well, when you try it out for yourself, you'll notice that after just a few minutes, you feel calmer and more grounded. Sometimes, all you need is to break the anxiety spiral and distract yourself long enough to calm down. The technique is often just what's needed to put the brakes on runaway anxiety.

You're also doing something else with this technique, and that is inviting your body to notice just how little danger there really is. Our minds can be screaming, "Danger, danger, danger! This is bad!", but if we pause a moment and check in with what is actually happening, we realize that things are . . . fine.

Sure, we may still have a problem to deal with, but we may be feeling far calmer and more in control about it than before. You can try this technique anywhere and at any time. You can even do it in public without people being aware that you're actively calming yourself down. If you're having a hard time and feel overwhelmed at work, for example, you can always excuse yourself to the bathroom and take a few minutes to gather yourself with this exercise.

One twist on the usual 5-4-3-2-1 exercise is to finish off with finding one positive thing about the present situation, or about yourself. Often, when we're lost in anxiety, we can feel like we're being ridiculous and getting worried over nothing, and this can leave us with a strong sense of embarrassment or even shame. Feeling so out of control can be a knock to the confidence and make us feel vulnerable and unsure of ourselves.

That's why it's so useful to ask yourself, "What good thing can I see in this situation right now?" or "What one good thing can I recognize in myself right now?" It may be that at the end of the exercise, you become aware of a possible solution, and that the problem doesn't seem so bad anymore. Maybe you simply remind yourself that you've been in tough situations before, and you've coped with it just fine. Or you realize that you have had the presence of mind and mental strength to recognize your anxiety and take control of the situation. Well done! You can feel proud about that!

2. HAVE A MANTRA

Being trapped in anxious overthinking can feel very lonely and scary, as though you're completely adrift. But really, you have plenty of anchors, emergency switches, and escape routes to help you halt the stress spiral and gain calm control again. One way you can put a speed bump in rumination is to use a mantra.

Mantras are a commonly overlooked form of meditation. Basically, a mantra is any word, phrase, or meaningless sound that you chant out loud in order to slow the mind, focus your thoughts, and come to awareness in the moment. Mantras have a long, religious, and devotional history in many different ancient cultures, but you needn't fully immerse yourself in the spiritual aspects to benefit from the mind-calming power of a mantra.

Many people find themselves overwhelmed or intimidated by meditation, and assume that it requires plenty of training or self-discipline. However, there are many different forms of meditation, and you can quickly learn to come to awareness and regain control of your mind without endless practice. Mantra meditations are intuitive, straightforward, and easy enough for anyone to master.

In 2016, Perry et. al. published a paper called "Chanting Meditation Improves Mood and Social Cohesion." In the researcher's experiment, they examined forty-five inexperienced chanters, as well as twenty-seven experienced chanters and discovered that simply chanting "om" for ten minutes can relieve anxiety and depression, focus the mind, boost mood, and even improve social bonding if done in a group.

A similar 2017 paper by Jai Dudeja wanted to understand the biochemical basis of this effect, suggesting that mantras may work because they boost the overall levels of nitric acid in the body, which regulates the nervous system, relaxes muscles, and increases blood flow. When we chant, we calm our autonomic nervous system and lower our breathing rate, our blood pressure, and our heart rate. And we breathe more deeply and slowly too!

What mantras should we use, and how?

First of all, classic Sanskrit mantras have very specific meanings, and you may or may not like to explore some of these. For example, the sound "om" is meant to evoke the primordial sound of creation itself, and chanting it is a contemplative practice on the nature of reality. Alternatively, you can use what's more commonly thought of in the West as an affirmation, and chant it like a mantra. Here are some excellent mantras in English that can help dissolve anxiety and worry:

- *This, too, shall pass,* (Reminds you that how you're feeling now won't last forever!)
- *One thing at a time,* (Just focus on what's in front of you, and you'll feel less overwhelmed,)
- *I am not my thoughts.* (To give some distance from negative self-talk.)
- *I'm only human.* (Mistakes are normal.)

- *I'm right here, right now.* (Reminds you to anchor in the present and in your body)
- You may simply like to repeat a calming word over and over, such as "peace, peace" or "om" which can be a profoundly calming and almost hypnotic sound
- You could also use a poem, a quote, a saying, or a favorite prayer that's personally meaningful to you
- You could use counting – either repeatedly count "one one one" or count up to three or five or ten over and over again. Some people find that counting *down* is somehow more relaxing.
- You can use a nonsense made-up phrase if you want to use mantras to simply distract an overwhelmed mind. Sometimes, it can help you realize that in a way, *all* your stressful thoughts and ruminations are just strings of meaningless sounds, too!

Once you've selected a mantra that you like, get comfortable, close your eyes, and take a few breaths. Arrive in the moment.

Now, start to repeat the mantra. You can repeat it mentally, whisper it, say it out loud, or even sing it. If possible, you could scribble it down or write it out, or connect the phrase to a bodily movement, such as walking. For example, every inhale represents three steps and the mantra *Let It Be*, each word connected to a step. You can then exhale again for the next three steps and repeat the mantra again. As you find a peaceful rhythm, your anxiety evaporates.

However you express the mantra, it's a good idea to find a consistent rhythm with your voice and breath, flowing smoothly and feeling your body rise and fall. Meditate on the sound itself. Immerse yourself in it fully, and become aware of your breath being shaped in your lungs and throat, and how the sound waves are leaving your body and going out into the world. You might like to recite the mantra on the inhale and exhale, or on the exhale only.

One option is to repeat the mantra, then taper it off. So, gradually lower your voice, then for a few repeats, simply move your lips without making sound. Finally, finish by repeating the mantra in your mind only. Imagine that as you open your eyes and carry on with the rest of your day, you are still internally carrying the essence of that mantra, keeping you serene and at peace.

This mantra meditation can be done at night before you go to sleep or in the morning as you prepare to take on your day. But it's also something you can use in the heat of the moment, so to speak. If you become aware of yourself feeling anxious, try to close your eyes, come to your breath and recite your mantra a few times. This can be especially effective if the mantra itself has been "mentally anchored" in the NLP fashion described above. This way, you can pair the movement of your lips, the sound of the mantra, and the associations of the words with a particular psychological state. Through the mantra, you can access this state whenever you want to.

3. SCAN YOUR BODY

We tend to think of anxiety as a psychological disorder, or something that's "all in your head." It isn't! The stress response has its roots in the ancient fight-or-flight mechanisms that begin in the brain and then manifest in the nervous and endocrine systems. In every organ and tissue of the body, in fact. This is why chronic stress can start to look like headaches, ongoing pain, allergies, digestive trouble . . . what began as a temporary state of autonomic arousal has lingered in the body and become illness.

There is nothing mystical, then, about saying that many pains and illnesses are simply anxieties trapped in the body. The relationship goes the other way, too, and we can experience our own *bodily* tensions and pains as *psychological* tensions and pains. In this way, our body and mind get caught in a reinforcing loop of anxiety. We feel stressed because our head hurts, but our head hurts because we feel stressed…

However, if we learn to scan our bodies and check in with ourselves regularly, we can notice small disruptions to our wellbeing early on before they become full-blown "dis-ease." We can bring awareness to what we're actually feeling, noticing our tiredness, the tightness in the back of our throat, or the pain in our lower back that says, "You've been working too long now without a break!"

Imagine your body works on this hierarchy:

Body > Emotion > Thought

For example, you could be overtired, a little dehydrated, and strung out on coffee (body). This state of arousal in your nervous system is associated with higher cortisol levels, for example, and so it's registered in your conscious awareness as stress, anxiety, or grumpiness (emotion). This emotion then instigates some higher-order thoughts, such as, "I suck at my job" (thought).

We may be used to interfacing with our experience only on this last level, ignoring the fact that the thoughts that we have emerge from how we feel, and how we feel emerges from our physical reality.

If we can become consciously aware of what is going on with us on *all* levels, we can take measures to relax ourselves and undo anxiety at its root. So, instead of dwelling on the question of our job and how much we hate it, we can tune into our emotions first and allow them to point us to the fact that we're overtired and dehydrated. The solution, you find out, has nothing to do with quitting your job—it's simply to give your body what it needs (rest, water) and find equilibrium again.

Doing a body scan is easy and can be done as often as you like, wherever you like. You can use the acronym CALM (or CLAM, if you're feeling funny) to help you remember the four main stress zones of the body to tune into.

C – Chest

A – Arms

L – Legs

M – Mouth

When you check in with these places, you get valuable information about your physical and emotional state. Plus, you get to consciously decide to relax these parts, which then causes your entire body and mind to release anxiety.

Start by finding a comfortable position and closing your eyes. Find your breath and slow down a little. Start with C, your chest. Imagine your consciousness is a scanning light running over every part of your chest, inside and outside. What sensations come to the top of your awareness? Notice everything you can. What is your breathing like? Notice its rate and depth. Notice any muscle tightness, pain, or tension. Remember that this notice is not judgment–you're not trying to catch yourself out or look for flaws or problems. Instead, try to imbue your attention with a sense of compassionate curiosity.

After you've checked in, it's time to relax this area. Take a few deep breaths (belly breaths, if you can) and notice how you feel. See if you can melt any tensions you've identified. Again, remember that "an effort to relax is a failure to relax." What this means is that you cannot force yourself to relax–it's a contradiction. What you can do is simply let go of the effort you are making to maintain tension, and allow that tension to be released, *passively*.

Let go. Imagine simply making no effort. Do nothing. When you feel like you're doing nothing, do even less. If it helps, imagine that you simply cannot even be bothered to hold any tension any more, and it's just falling out of your body.

Next, move on to A, your arms. This includes the top of your shoulders and all the way down to your fingertips. Is there any movement and tension there? Maybe you notice your palms are sweaty or your fists clenched. To relax this area, squeeze your hands into fists and tense up the entire arm, then slowly release again with your exhale. Do this a few times, feeling the stretch and the release deepen each time. You might like to imagine that tension is releasing from your body in the form of a fine mist–once it evaporates, imagine it's gone forever and simply has no existence anymore.

Next, scan L, your legs. Do the same here, looking for tension and then deliberately relaxing the area. Tense the muscles, then gradually release the tension again. This is called progressive muscle relaxation. Relaxing from the most activated state actually results in a deeper release. Finally end with M, your mouth, which can hold a surprising amount of tension. Notice your jaw, your tongue, your lips. Zoom in on the sensations inside and outside. To relax this area, let everything hang a little looser, let the tension melt away, and if you like, allow your lips to come to a soft and relaxed smile.

As you complete the above exercise, you might notice something: the awareness of physical sensations easily blends into awareness of emotional sensations. That's because our emotions have their basis in the body. For example, the fluttery, nauseous feeling at the center of your chest feels like panic and self-doubt. The hollow wobbly feeling in the pit of your stomach is shame. The tight band of tension around the top of your head is overwhelm. And so on.

As you scan your body, see if it is communicating anything to you. If your chest, arms, etc. could speak, what would they say? What emotions do they each hold? By asking these questions, you develop physiological and emotional awareness at the same time, and you strengthen your mind-body connection. You may even start to see how your anxious thoughts and rumination actually begin in this embodied emotion.

Dr. Lauri Nummenmaa studied seven hundred people and actually mapped out the places in the body where people most consistently experience certain emotions. By asking people to self-report where they experienced certain emotions on a body map, she discovered how consistent the responses were.

For example, anger was most often felt in the hands and head, while disgust centered around the mouth. The fascinating results were published in a 2013 paper in the journal *Proceedings of The National Academy of Sciences.* Dr. Paul Zak of Claremont Graduate University says that the "areas in the brain that process emotions tend to be largely outside of our conscious awareness" and that we can't really know how our body is processing emotions. Nevertheless, we can still increase our awareness of what it is possible to be aware of, and we can still calm and relax ourselves, even if we lack perfect understanding of the underlying mechanisms.

You can learn to use your body to explore your thoughts and emotions. You'll be able to spot emotions emerging in yourself more quickly, and this means you give yourself the choice of how you want to respond—consciously.

You can adapt the body scan to fit your needs. You don't need to use the CALM acronym. You could simply scan yourself from head to toe, or ask your body to show you what it most wants to communicate. One great practice is to finish your scan with perceiving the entire body as a whole all at once. This heightens your mind-body awareness and gives you real insights into your overall emotional state. See how long you can hold on to this heightened awareness as you go about the rest of your day.

4. LAUGHTER MEDITATION

Laughter meditation—is that when you make yourself laugh? Yes! And it's as cheesy and ridiculous as it sounds. Luckily, cheesy and ridiculous are exactly what we're going for. Laughter is medicine. It's also good fun and, paradoxically, the sillier it is, the more effective. As a form of meditation, it's easy and straightforward, as there is nothing to achieve and no goal to focus on or anything to visualize. You just laugh, and you do it for no reason at all. If only all medicine was that sweet, huh?

Developed by Dr. Madan Kataria, this is definitely an underrated mindfulness practice. The idea is that when you are laughing, your anxious mind cannot run all over the place. You are completely and utterly in the present and in your body—and that's what meditation is all about. So far, we've explored many different things to displace anxiety with–deep breathing, gratitude, body awareness, a mantra. In this chapter, we'll look at how the full-body experience of laughter is a little like a combination of all of these, and is particularly good at chasing away anxious states of mind.

Does it feel strange and awkward to start? Yes. We're used to laughing in response to something. But we *can* laugh whenever we like—and humans are the only animals that can! Laughter lowers stress, improves immune function, and enhances your digestion. Laughter doesn't just engage the whole body, but it brings about an enormous sense of emotional and cognitive relief, and seems to drastically reframe our entire attitude.

Laughing lowers cortisol levels in the body, but it does so much more than this. After a big belly laugh, don't you find yourself feeling more tolerant, accepting, relaxed, and open-minded? Big egos deflate, emergencies seem more manageable, and joy bubbles to the surface. It's as though all the things that seemed so deadly serious and threatening a moment ago have shrunk in size and just don't seem to bother you as much.

A 2011 paper published in *Science Direct* by Ramon Mora-Ripoll found that so-called "simulated laughter" can work as both a preventative for general wellbeing, and as a kind of medicine to treat things like anxiety and depression. The review also discovered that the laughter prescription is one of the few interventions that has virtually no side effects—so you have nothing to lose by trying it!

A 2016 paper by Louie et. al. had similar findings, noting that laughter actually has an analgesic (pain relief) effect. They explore the MCET—the "Motion Creates Emotion Theory"—in other words, if you go through the motions of laughing, you actually create a genuine sense of fun and humor in yourself. So, don't worry too much about "real" or "fake" laughter—your body can't tell the difference, and in fact, fake laughter often turns into real laughter anyway.

So how do you practice laughter meditation?

The best time is in the morning on an empty stomach. Begin by stretching, taking time to loosen up the muscles in your mouth, jaw, and face. Practice smiling. Start small and begin to see how this smile spreads into the other muscles of your face. Start laughing, but don't force anything. Just imagine it flowing out of you.

You're not laughing **at** anything, but rather laughing **with** it. Whatever emerges in your experience, laugh at it. Keep this up for a while. With a little practice, you may find that you're actually able to make yourself have big, full belly laughs—yes, really! When you're done, allow the laughter to fade as gently as it started. Gradually come to stillness again in your body, feeling the warm smile on your face and the good feelings in your body. Find stillness again. Finish the meditation by standing up and having a nice stretch. Let thoughts flutter past you and simply dwell on the sensations in your body. With regular practice, laughter meditation can have powerful effects on your life and banish anxiety.

If you're feeling adventurous, you can seek out a group to practice laughter meditation with. The awkwardness is initially greater, but you may find you reach that mindful state a lot quicker. You will be forced to not take yourself or the activity too seriously. Just access that inner child, be silly, and don't worry about how it all pans out. Meditation, then, can be thought of as play. Completely pointless and a lot of fun. And that's all. Why not?

It probably can't hurt to include more humor and laughter in your life more generally. Seek out comedy and funny shows or clips, make jokes and pull pranks, or simply try to see the silly side of life. Lots of people find benefit in creating their own curated lists of funny clips and videos to watch when they're feeling low. Think of it as a comedy medicine cabinet to quickly help you shift your mental state and shake off any accumulated tension. Remember that it doesn't matter if it's considered groan-inducing or embarrassing to anyone else–in fact, the more ludicrous, the better.

Laughing at yourself is an incredibly powerful way to melt anxiety knots. Arguing and fighting against stress just makes more stress—but what if you just laugh at it? The next time you're in a big, serious mental tangle and worrying over this or that, try to zoom out and take another perspective. Can you see how silly it all is? How silly *you* are?

5. LOVING-KINDNESS MEDITATION

Let's move on to another very accessible form of meditation that never loses its effectiveness: loving kindness. This kind of meditation (often shortened to LKM) is the perfect way to cultivate compassion in ourselves, and improves not only our relationships with others but with ourselves. It can also work wonders for the stressed-out and anxious mind. This kind of activity is particularly beneficial for those of us whose anxiety tends to take on a tone of judgement, condemnation, shame or blame. These negative states of mind have a strong overlap with anxiety.

Do you recognize yourself in any of the following?

- After social events, you find yourself ruminating over what people said, what they thought of you or, conversely, what you thought of them.
- You dwell on past disagreements, fights, or arguments with others and the resulting unresolved tensions.
- You judge and criticize others or, on the other hand, constantly worry that others are judging and criticizing you.
- You find it hard to forgive others or yourself.
- Your anxious ruminations are often tinged with blame and condemnation of others, or else with shame and guilt about what you have and haven't done.
- Your anxiety seems to make it harder to connect with other people, to empathize, understand, or accommodate them.
- You feel superior to others, or inferior... or both!

While most people today are familiar with the concept of stress and anxiety, few of us can appreciate the *social* dimension of our own anxiety. In other words, our anxiety can often be both a cause and a symptom of poor relationships with others. We may experience anxiety because we are too harsh and unforgiving with ourselves or others, cannot forgive our enemies, find it hard to accept flaws in ourselves and others, and allow judgment and criticism to create tension.

Loving kindness meditation is a way to promote deep and lasting compassion, but it also has the surprising side effect of allowing all of this social anxiety to dissipate, too. During this meditation, we practice focusing kind and benevolent energy toward other people and toward ourselves. It's a technique that is simple, but not always easy. Sending and receiving love can be challenging!

A 2018 review in the *Harvard Review of Psychology* by Graser and Stangier collected an impressive amount of scientific evidence for LKM (as well as other types of meditation). According to the researchers, "LKM was effective in treating chronic pain and (. . .) borderline personality disorder. A larger number of nonrandomized studies indicate that (. . .) LKM may be effective in treating a wide range of clinical conditions, including depression, anxiety disorders, chronic pain, and posttraumatic stress disorder."

Other studies have found that LKM can improve marriages, soothe social anxiety, reduce anger, improve empathy, and help with forgiveness (Totzeck et. al. 2020; Zeng et. al. 2015). LKM can also:

- Increase gray matter in the area of the brain associated with emotional regulation (Leung et. al., 2012).
- Boost life satisfaction, and increase feelings of awe, gratitude, pride, and hope (Fredrickson et. al., 2011).
- Make you more likely to help others and be generous (Klimecki et. al., 2013).

Though there are many variations, and you can adjust the approach as you see fit, the general process goes a little something like this:

Step 1: Find some time in your day when you won't be distracted, and sit or lie somewhere comfortable, eyes closed. Find your breath and relax a little.

Step 2: Imagine someone you love dearly. Picture their face. Feel the love and kindness as a glow inside you and dwell on these feelings for a moment. You can visualize this kindness and compassion as a bright light or similar, or you can quietly chant the words, "May you be happy. May you be safe and at peace." Imagine yourself holding this person in a cocoon of light in your heart. However you picture it, the idea is to conjure up strong feelings of love and kindness.

Step 3: Holding on to this warm fuzzy feeling, imagine someone else—someone you like, but do not love. Try to project this same loving-kindness onto them. See the humanity in this person. See how they have hopes and dreams and fears. How they were once innocent children. How they, too, hold the spark of the divine within them. "May you be happy. May you be safe and at peace."

Step 4: Move your attention again, this time to someone you're neutral about. Can you feel kindness and compassion for them, too? Can you see how they love as deeply as you do? And that even if you don't know them fully, can you see that deep inside they are a beautiful being who deserves compassion and kindness?

Step 5: Keep shifting your attention. Find someone you dislike a little. This can be difficult, but try to imagine holding them in the same light as you held your loved ones. Even if you don't like them—even if you hate them— can you still find a little well of goodwill for them anyway? Not because they "deserve" it, but . . . just because?

Step 6: Finally, take the step that some people find hardest of all: extend your warm glow of loving-kindness to yourself. Drop the desire to label, to judge, to find fault. Just look at yourself in all your flawed and beautiful humanity and imagine bathing yourself in a warm, glowing light of kindness.

Step 7: When you're ready, come out of your meditation, take a few deep breaths, stretch, and continue with your day.

Practice this for a few minutes every day and be prepared to be astonished at how much your life changes. You will find relaxation and calm, yes, but you will also discover other benefits. So many people who battle anxiety are very hard on themselves. But in LKM, we smile kindly on this and accept it. You are just right just as you are. And other people are just right, too. There is no problem, and nothing to fight against. And so, anxiety can dissolve. Look at others and really try to feel that they are doing their best. Look inward and understand that your anxiety is only trying to help you, and that just because you are not a perfect human being, it doesn't mean you don't deserve understanding and kindness.

If you're the kind of person whose anxiety focuses on other people (social situations, relationships, guilt, etc.), this can be a powerful way to relinquish control. Love and anxiety don't exist together. Fill your heart with warmth and acceptance, and you're far less likely to notice problems or to slip into fearful resistance. What's more, you can find forgiveness—for yourself and others. Why ruminate on what's already been done? Let it go in forgiveness. Not because you agree with it or condone it, but because deep down all you want is peace and happiness for yourself and others. Doesn't that feel so, so much better than anxiety?

That warm glow inside your heart is always there. Practice repeatedly tuning into it, and you'll find it almost impossible to be anxious!

Summary:

- Mindfulness techniques are a proven and effective way to combat anxiety, stress, and overthinking, but you don't have to do formal sitting meditation to get the benefits.
- One easy technique is to take a few minutes to practice deep belly breathing to oxygenate and relax your body.
- Another is to use the 5-4-3-2-1 grounding technique to come back into your body and

the present moment by tuning into all five senses. You could finish by seeking out something positive about the situation or yourself.

- Chanting a mantra is another accessible mindfulness technique. Try saying an affirmation aloud, or just internally to distract and calm yourself.
- Do a body scan in the morning to check in with how you're feeling and correct any minor tensions before they become strong negative emotions and anxious thoughts. Use the CALM acronym to scan Chest, Arms, Legs, and Mouth, scan from head to toe, or simply ask your body what it wants to communicate to you. Use progressive muscle relaxation to loosen any tension you find.
- Laughter meditation takes a little bravery, but can flood you with feel-good hormones and banish stress and anxiety, whether practiced alone or in a group.
- Try loving kindness meditation to calm social anxiety, and learn to be a little kinder and compassionate with yourself.

Chapter 4. The First Step is Seeing It

The thing about visualization is that you are already an expert at it! Many people think they don't have much capacity for visualization, or feel that their imaginations are not especially well-developed, but the truth is that whenever you stress and ruminate and worry, visualization is exactly what you're doing! You are creating distressing mental pictures that then cause an adverse reaction in your body. If you've ever been worried about something, then guess what? You are a master visualizer and what's more, you already know about the power of investing your visualizations with *belief.*

So, why not use this ability your brain already possesses and put it to better use? In this chapter, we're looking at scientifically proven ways to use the power of your imagination to calm anxiety, gain psychological distance, and learn to exteriorize your experience.

1. GUIDED IMAGERY

Guided imagery is a straightforward stress management tool that helps you relax. You simply imagine, in vivid detail, peaceful settings or situations. The results, however, are very far from simple.

To illustrate, try right now to think of a super sour lemon in great detail. Close your eyes and imagine yourself biting into one. Really imagine the cold, waxy peel and the zing of the acidic lemony taste on your tongue and on your teeth. Can you imagine a tight, clenching feeling at the back of your jaw? Can you picture one eye twitching slightly closed as the sourness tingles on your tastebuds? Think of the lemon for long enough and you'll start to salivate!

It's the same with guided imagery. When it comes to stress and relaxation, your brain cannot tell the difference between imagined and real. So, when you imagine peaceful things, your body responds physically and releases feel-good hormones. This is why guided imagery has been associated with reduced stress and better relaxation.

A study published in 2014 (Menzies et. al., *Journal of Behavioral Medicine*) took women suffering from fibromyalgia and put them into two groups. One group did guided imagery exercises every day for ten weeks, while the other group didn't. At the end of the ten-week period, the women who did the guided imagery reported significant drops in their pain, stress, fatigue, and depression levels.

Another study (Patricolo et. al., 2017) did something similar, but compared the effects of guided imagery with those of clinical massage. The participants were patients in a progressive care unit. The results? Thirty minutes of guided imagery had the same effect on the participants as fifteen minutes of therapeutic massage. Guided imagery has also been shown to reduce pain, improve sleep quality, relieve fatigue, and improve depression.

Practicing guided imagery is easy, and there are so many ways to do it. You can try it when you wake up, before you sleep, or as part of a yoga practice or meditation session. You can use an audio recording or app to help you, make your own recording, or be creative and guide yourself. Take a look at YouTube or download one of the countless apps now available. The general process goes as follows:

- Sit somewhere quiet and get comfortable. Close your eyes and relax your breathing.
- You could start with any breathing exercise you like or do a little stretching to loosen your muscles.
- Now, in your mind's eye, take the time to imagine a peaceful, relaxing place. Your imagination is the limit: you could visualize an epic and serene mountain range in the snow, a heavenly garden with a palace made of crystal at its center, or a cozy library with a warm crackling fire in the corner. You could also think of a place from your memory.
- Now, don't rush. In as vivid detail as possible, imagine all the elements of this scene using all five senses. The smell of the sea breeze. The sound of children laughing. The sight of sunlight glittering through the tops of the trees . . . Don't forget to imagine how you feel in this place, too. What are you wearing? What are you doing and thinking?

- How you interact with this scene is up to you. You can walk through a path you create in your imagination, or simply imagine yourself at the center of a tranquil picture and notice what comes and goes. Some people imagine an enormous healing pool with a stone staircase that lowers you step by step into the magical water. Others imagine a stately museum that they browse through room by room.
- As you sink into your visualization, keep your breathing slow and regular and let go of any ideas of what you should be doing. Your only goal is to indulge in the relaxation you are creating for yourself.
- When you're done, take a deep breath, stretch, and open your eyes.

As you can see, there's plenty of leeway for you to make guided imagery your own. It's a good idea, though, to make sure you won't be disturbed (i.e., turn your phone to silent!) and wear comfy clothing. If imagining scenes is difficult at first, don't worry—you will get better with practice. You may find it helpful to first study images and photographs of gorgeous locations. Then close your eyes and imagine you're really there. What else can you see when you explore just outside the frame?

Don't worry if visualization seems like hard work at first. Each of us visualizes things in a unique way–it's just a matter of learning what works for you. A great way to practice visualization is to first try to imagine ordinary things in your world. For example, close your eyes and imagine coming home and opening your front door. This shouldn't be difficult, as you've probably done it hundreds of times before. Just imagine the color of the door, the feeling of the handle in your hands, the texture of the mat or step beneath you...

Once you feel comfortable doing this, you can then work to extend your imaginative power by introducing more elements (can you walk into your home and move through the rooms of your house in turn?) or something brand new (what if the door was painted a different color? What if there was a parcel at the door?). In time, you'll flex your visualization muscle and strengthen your ability to deliberately conjure up mental imagery according to your own will.

You can use audio recordings and prompts at first, but you may find you're able to go deeper once you take your time and create your own mental image. One great thing to do is create a mental sanctuary that you can repeatedly return to. In a way, this place acts like a "mental anchor" as we explored earlier. Your body and mind come to associate this place with deep relaxation. Every time you "visit," you can add another little detail.

Why not combine mantras with your imagery? This way, even if you don't have time to go into a full visualization session, you can evoke some of the associated emotions just by reciting your mantra. For example, in a stressful moment during the day, you can close your eyes, take a deep breath, and say, "Cool wet grass," to remind you of your inner safe space. It's amazing how suggestible your brain can be, and how quickly you can change your emotional state!

2. METAPHORIZE YOUR ANXIETY

Earlier in this book, we explored the subtle power of labelling our emotions and experiences, and the increased psychological distance this could create for us. If you've been practicing this, you may have already discovered that one way to expand on this concept is to use a metaphor or simile to express how we're feeling. For example, you could describe your state of mind as "terrified", but also say, "I feel as though I'm clinging onto a rope for dear life, but with each second the rope is breaking a little more and at any moment it'll snap completely and I'll fall into a dark abyss below..."

When we use metaphors, we not only increase our emotional literacy, self-awareness, and expression, but we also gain that precious psychological distance between us and whatever is bothering us. We become observers of our feelings rather than slaves to them. Your brain really is an amazing organ, and with a little prompting, you can use it to completely reshape your experience and the relationship you have with your anxiety.

In fact, the idea of having a "relationship with anxiety" is itself a metaphor! It's a metaphor that helps you see anxiety as something that can be understood and collaborated with.

Metaphors can help us describe how we're feeling, but they can also be used proactively, as tools that allow us to deliberately alter our state of mind. The right metaphor can open up brand new perspectives. Here are some useful ones you can incorporate into your own practice:

Clouds in the sky

A popular Buddhist conception of anxiety (and all sensation and thought) is that they are like clouds moving across a sky. We are the sky—blue, depthless, eternal. But the weather is always changing. It comes, it goes. Anxiety is like this. It comes and it goes. It's like weather.

When we explore this metaphor, we start to see anxiety not as a problem to solve, but as something as harmless and fleeting as passing clouds. Do you get angry at clouds? Do you fight against them or twist yourself into a knot figuring out how to "solve" them? They don't need to be solved. They come, and then they go.

In this metaphor, identifying with the clouds means your experience is fragmented, changing, and distressing, but what if you identify with the unchanging blue behind the clouds?

New perspective: Even if right now you are anxious, it doesn't mean you always will be. Life is always changing, but you are who you are. You can embrace what is. You don't have to fight with it.

Waves in the ocean

Founder of Mindfulness Based Stress Reduction (MBSR) Jon Kabat-Zinn once said, "You can't stop the waves, but you can learn to surf." This is not dissimilar to the previous metaphor–we can see the waves of life around us as simply movement in the field. What is the difference between squeezing your eyes shut and letting the body of the wave smash into you at full force, versus jumping up when the wave comes, and floating along the top of it, i.e. "going with the flow"?

What is the difference between stressfully berating yourself by saying, "Just calm down already! Whatever you do just CALM DOWN!" versus realizing that you're anxious, accepting the anxiety, and choosing to just get on with life anyway? In other words, what happens to anxiety when you are no longer anxious about it?

New perspective: We can't control anxiety. But we can roll with it. We are able to cope with anything that comes our way.

Trains on a platform

You are the station, and thoughts arrive as trains, each one taking you to a different destination. There are a lot of trains, and the chaos and noise can be overwhelming, but remember: you only have to board one at a time, and you can choose which train you hop on. If you want, you can just sit there and watch a train come, and go right on by. It can go ahead to its destination, without you on it.

So, someone could cut you off in traffic and you could instantly feel the rising anger and indignation within you, but you could instead become aware and read the sign: "Boarding now: one-way train to Rageville." What does it feel like to consciously choose to just let those feelings dissipate, without grabbing hold of them? We don't *have to* react.

New perspective: Just because a thought is there doesn't mean we have to "board" it and follow where it goes. We can watch it come and leave the station without us on it!

A grumpy two-year-old

Your anxiety isn't a fearsome demon set out to torture you for all eternity. It's not ultra-powerful. It's just an annoying, but completely manageable two-year-old who will calm down eventually. You can't ignore a tantrum, but you know that getting upset won't fix anything. Just talk kindly and patiently with the two-year-old and wait for the drama to pass. Forgive the anxiety—it's just afraid and overwhelmed. It's doing its best.

Whenever your brain starts getting carried away with "what if" thoughts, understand that you are occupying a particular perspective. Change that perspective a little and things won't seem as threatening.

You could imagine your anxiety as a tornado (crazy on the inside, but relatively calm if you just step out of the center) or a box of worries that you can open at will or store away somewhere safe when you're tired of worrying. You could imagine that you have a soul bank account filled with life units, and every time you worry, you spend one unit of life that you could have spent on something that could make you happy instead.

Whichever metaphor you go with, it should be something that really speaks to you in a meaningful way. When you notice yourself drifting off into a "sea of anxiety," call up the image of waves. When you notice that critical and negative self-talk dominating your thoughts, imagine a little dial that you can turn to lower the volume so you can hear the rest of life.

Try the "leaves on a stream exercise"

One potent visualization/metaphor exercise is called "leaves on a stream." This is a "cognitive defusion" technique that is used in ACT—Action Commitment Therapy—and is designed to help you get distance from uncomfortable or overwhelming feelings. The shift in perspective is similar to the one we achieve when we metaphorize our anxiety: we realize, "I am having thoughts, but I am not my thoughts."

Here's how to do this simple practice.

- First, sit comfortably somewhere you won't be disturbed, breathing deeply. You know the drill!
- Next, picture yourself sitting beside a tranquil, flowing stream. In this stream are some fallen leaves peacefully floating by . . .
- As a thought pops into your mind, see it there, pick it up, and place it gently onto a passing leaf. Watch it float by out of your field of vision as the stream flows on.
- Do this with ALL your thoughts. Stressful, neutral, blissful. Put them all on the leaves and watch them go.

Now, you're not trying to dispose of thoughts or get rid of them. You're not rushing the stream along or trying to slow it. If you have a thought like, "This stream exercise is dumb," then simply pick that up, too, and put it on a leaf. If you think, "I'm really doing well with this," then yes, you guessed it, put it on a leaf too. Easy. If your mind wanders and you get sidetracked, it's no big deal. Just come back to your task with the leaves and carry on without admonishing yourself or feeling bad.

3. TALK ABOUT YOURSELF IN THIRD PERSON

Why does talking to other people about our worries make us feel better? Even if the problem isn't solved, we still feel some relief. What helps may simply be the fact that talking about our problems is a way to externalize and abstract our worry, putting some distance between it and ourselves. The great thing is, though, that you don't have to literally talk to a friend to experience these benefits. If you can learn to talk about yourself in third person, you still achieve that sense of distance and objectivity.

This is yet another way we can switch perspective and gain some relief from rumination and worry. What happens when you switch your point of view and think of yourself as a friend would think of you? What would happen if you spoke to yourself as if you were speaking to someone you knew (who had your name and all your problems) and who was asking for your help and advice?

A study published in 2017 in *Scientific Reports* by professor of psychology Jason Moser and his colleagues asked these very questions. The researchers found that talking about yourself as though you were someone else can help you relieve strong negative emotions. All you have to do is stop using "I" statements and instead use "he," "she," or "you." So, instead of saying, "I'm having a panic attack," you say, "She's having a panic attack," or, "Anna is having a panic attack."

It doesn't seem like that big of a deal, but Moser's research shows that when people do this, they self-report lower levels of anxiety. Again, we see the power of psychological distance. "By using your own name, and possibly also second-person pronouns, it creates this little separation from the self. It makes you think about your feelings and thoughts like you're looking at somebody else's experience," says Moser.

One experiment went like this. Participants looked at stock images and videos from upsetting news stories, then were asked to think about what they saw, first using the first-person point of view ("I was saddened") and then using third person ("Jay thought this was sad").

Simply by using their own names to talk about themselves, the participants showed more activity in the parts of the brain associated with emotional regulation. The emotion is still there, of course. It's just not as *close*. What's more, using third person takes no more effort than using first person, so it's a great tool to use on the spot when you're feeling overwhelmed.

Imagine you've just heard some very stressful news—a family member has had a serious car accident and is in the hospital, and you've had a panicky phone call from your mother. Your head suddenly explodes into dozens of different thoughts, and you're instantly overwhelmed. You know you should probably ask your boss if you can take some time off work so you can head over to the ER and do what you can, but you notice yourself quickly getting strung out as you start to panic, too. "What if I'm so stressed that *I* have a car accident on the way over? What if I get there too late and everyone is disappointed in me? What if my boss gets unhappy about me taking time off? What am I going to do?!"

Instead, ask yourself, "What is Michael going to do?" Can you instantly see how this takes so much of the panic out of the equation? It's as though you are looking at a movie of yourself from the outside in. Suddenly the stakes aren't as high. You can see a solution or a way forward.

Psychology professor Ethan Kross, who is also director at the Emotion and Self Control Lab, conducted a similar experiment. He asked participants to think about upsetting memories from the past, but to do so using third-person language. While they did this, their brain activity was examined using fMRI. They showed reduced activity in the parts of the brain we know are connected to the experience of pain. In other words, Kross found evidence that talking about painful memories in the third person reduces how painful they feel.

"What's really exciting here is that (…) third-person self-talk may constitute a relatively effortless form of emotion regulation. If this ends up being true—we won't know until more research is done—there are lots of important implications these findings have for our basic understanding of how self-control works, and for how to help people control their emotions in daily life," Kross said.

We don't have to wait for further research to be done, however, to get some benefit from making small tweaks to our language. Of course, you don't have to speak like this permanently. Rather, use the third-person trick to defuse especially stressful moments and take the edge off. You only need to do it long enough to gain some distance. Just momentarily take on a different perspective and see if that releases some of the tension. From there, you can take action or choose to let your worry go.

4. ROLE-PLAYING

You're probably familiar with role-playing in general, but did you know that role-playing is a useful tool when it comes to managing anxiety? You can use role-play to rehearse and prepare for difficult conversations or situations. When you role-play, you are exploring potential ways of behaving, finding new approaches and perspectives, and accessing new insights—all while staying in control. Role-playing can also be combined with many of the other approaches we've looked at—like naming how you feel, gaining distance by using third-person language, and being more self-aware.

How can we use role-play to help with stress and tension? First, identify a situation that's causing some anxiety for you. Let's say you're ruminating over a difficult conversation you need to have with a family member. Now, instead of endlessly turning the problem over in your head and causing stress, try to make the issue *concrete*—play out the possible conversation and see what happens. Maybe you enlist the help of a trusted friend or even a therapist. You sit together and try to make the situation feel as real as possible.

Assign the roles you'll each play. For example, if you wanted to clarify your thoughts and squash nervousness, you could play yourself and they could play the family member. Then you could practice the conversation. If you reverse this order, however, you might see different sides to the story and gain fresh insight and empathy into how the family member might be feeling.

Act out the conversation. Notice any anxiety or nerves. Notice how you feel afterward. Notice if anything changes after you start talking and once the conversation is finished. Is there some aspect of the issue you hadn't considered before? Even though role-playing this way can feel awkward to start with, it's actually a brilliant way to turbo-charge your communication skills.

There are many ways to use role-playing when it comes to overthinking and rumination:

- You could rehearse a job interview
- You could practice staying calm and focused during conversations where

there may be some conflict to resolve—for example, during a meeting with an angry client
- You could rehearse a "performance," whether that's literally on a stage or a presentation at work, a wedding speech or a first date. Being prepared in advance will help you feel confident in yourself
- You could use role-playing to help you better understand a social situation, testing out possible outcomes and seeing how you'll react. Role-playing can boost empathy and help you get into other people's heads
- You could use role-play to desensitize yourself to fears and phobias. For example, those with social anxiety can practice small talk and introducing themselves, even "rewinding" and trying different tactics to get a feel for it in a safe and low-stakes way

Often, anxiety grows in the face of the unknown. But when you role-play, you are actively grappling with that unknown. You take your fears and worries and put them outside your head where you can work on them productively. You can take the stress-inducing "what if" statements and literally try them out.

When you're anxious, your brain believes that something is more dangerous and threatening than it is. But with role-play, you can prove to yourself that the situation is actually manageable. Scared of monsters under the bed? Well, go with a friend and see for yourself if there's anything there!

One way to approach role-playing is to **start with a fear or threat**. What scares or overwhelms you? Maybe you say "germs" or "busy social situations."

Next, think of your current behavior and attitude, then **imagine a new behavior** or mindset that you'd like to practice. For example, you'd like to be more comfortable and relaxed around meeting new people at parties.

Now, think of ways to **recreate this "threatening" situation**. With a therapist or friend (pick one who is good at acting!), run through some potentially stressful situations. Maybe you most hate those first few moments when you meet someone new and you're struggling to think of what to say. So, practice that over and over. Have the other person pretend to be a stranger and meet them, trying out this new behavior you want to learn.

Don't worry about making mistakes—in fact, messing things up and seeing that it's not the end of the world is all part of it! Think of it as teaching yourself that the threat is not a threat after all.

Gradually **dial up the intensity**. Once you're feeling confident in small talk from a cold start, see what it's like to talk to someone who is actively rude or uninterested. You may find that with enough practice, you actually start enjoying yourself. If you can start to see it all as a game, you know that the role-playing is working!

Naturally, not every anxiety or worry is going to translate into a role-play exercise. And let's be honest, many of us won't have someone we can practice with. But that doesn't mean you can't still benefit from this approach! Simply try *mentally rehearsing* a certain situation. Walk your brain step by step through a threatening scenario and practice what you say, what you feel, what you do, and what you think.

If you like, you can mix things up, too. Try to mentally rehearse the roles of other people in a scenario and see if that perspective shift shines new light on the problem. Or get abstract and role-play with your anxiety itself.

Imagine it's sitting in a chair in front of you and literally talk to it. "Anxiety, what are you trying to achieve here? What are you worried about?" Make friends and try to come to a compromise. Sounds cheesy, but when you take the role of your own ultra-wise mentor/therapist, you'd be surprised at what you're capable of!

5. HAVE AN ALTER EGO

Kids who were instructed to imagine that they were Batman ended up having greater perseverance in a difficult task than kids who didn't. That's the finding of a fascinating 2016 study conducted by White et. al. at the University of Minnesota. Coining this phenomenon "the Batman effect," the researchers noted that merely pretending you are someone who is brave, capable, and strong can actually make you perform better.

The idea is that if you can take on the perspective of someone who is stronger and more proficient than yourself, then you literally allow yourself to reflect on a challenge in an entirely different way. Again, we see the power of creating psychological distance. If you can imagine how a person other than you would respond in a situation, you give yourself access to that same response.

In the study, the researchers asked kids who were four to six years old to do a task for ten minutes. They were also offered the chance to break up this task with an appealing video game. The kids who were told to simulate a strong role model actually ended up working harder and longer on the task than other kids. In this experiment, the other groups were told to take a third-person perspective ("Johnny is trying to figure out this puzzle") or an ordinary first-person perspective.

The study showed us that a mental role model could help children with self-discipline, focus, and perseverance. But it can also help adults emulate other characteristics they are trying to develop. Many famous musicians and performers have such an alter ego: even if they have stage fright and low self-confidence, their alter ego doesn't. When on stage, they do what their alter ego would do. Beyonce is said to use her alter ego (called "Sasha") to help her be what she wants to be on stage.

If we think of anxiety as a pattern of thought and behavior, we can think of alter egos as a way to "try on" a completely different pattern. It's difficult to step out of your own character at times, but it's easy to imagine another character. Think about a person who is relaxed, confident, and easy going. Imagine what a strong, self-assured, and in-control person thinks, says, and does. They may be a real person, a fictional character, or an imaginary person of your own creation.

The next time you're feeling anxious or overwhelmed, set your own ego aside for a moment and look at the situation from your alter ego's perspective. Do you remember the "What Would Jesus Do?" bangles that were popular in the 90s? The same principle applies. Granted, you might not always feel up to being as brave or relaxed as your alter ego, but the point is to at least entertain that perspective. The more you identify with that alter ego, the more you close the gap between how you are now and how you'd like to be.

Let's recap some simple steps to unlocking the "Batman effect" for yourself:

1. Think of something in yourself you'd like to work on—for example, your pessimistic self-talk or tendency to catastrophize.
2. Now, invert this. What does the opposite look like? You might decide it's a person who consistently and cheerfully assumes the best and always sees the silver lining.

3. Now construct an alter ego who possesses this characteristic in buckets. They could have other characteristics, too, or you might like to have a different alter ego for each characteristic. You could flesh them out by giving them a name, an appearance, and so on. Have fun with it. Maybe you're socially anxious and your confident and popular alter ego is called "Catherine the Great."
4. The next time you're facing any challenge or obstacle, ask what your alter ego would do. What would they feel in this situation? Really dwell in their perspective. Then do what they'd do.

Here's how that might look. Let's say you are someone who constantly overthinks things. You decide you'd like to tackle your tendency to stew over minor details and make yourself stressed. You turn this tendency upside down and imagine an alter ego who is happy-go-lucky, calm, confident, and doesn't take things too seriously. This alter ego is a blend of someone you once knew and admired, a fictional character you read about in a book, and someone entirely made up. You call this person Eddie (because he's a bit like Eddie

Murphy) and flesh out how he looks and acts. He's always smiling, and he likes to go with the flow, have fun, and see what happens.

One day you're planning a vacation and you notice your overthinking, stressed-out self appearing. You stop and think, *what would Eddie do?* Actually, Eddie would laugh at all this planning. Why so serious? Half the fun is going and figuring out what you want to do on the fly, right? Live life. Be a little spontaneous. Through Eddie's eyes, your nine-page-long Excel itinerary looks a little silly. You laugh at yourself, and when you next think about your upcoming vacation, you speak in his voice as you tell yourself, "I don't know what we're doing when we get there, but it'll be fun finding out!"

Summary:

- The imagination is a powerful thing and can be put to use to help combat anxiety and quell overthinking. Guided imagery, for example, is a great way to imagine a peaceful scenario in enough detail that our body responds by relaxing.
- Another effective stress management technique is to use metaphors to help you alter your relationship to anxiety and think of it in a different way. You could imagine

that stress is like clouds passing by in the sky, passing trains, or a restless toddler.

- You can also gain this psychological distance by talking about yourself and your anxiety in the third person (for example, "David is worried about this" when talking about yourself).
- Role-play exercises are another way to use the power of visualizing. Literally act out and rehearse anxiety-provoking scenarios with a friend or therapist, or try to practice situations in your mind to de-sensitize you and help you feel more prepared and confident.
- Finally, create an alter ego for yourself who possesses the opposite of some stressful characteristics you want to be free of. Flesh out this alter ego and allow yourself to take on their perspective as your own when you're faced with a challenging or stressful situation.

Chapter 5. Reframe and Shift

In our final chapter, we're taking a closer look at a few key shifts in attitude that can drastically alter your perspective and help you think differently about your anxiety. If you've been applying some of the techniques and methods already discussed, you may notice for yourself a subtle shift in your own attitude and mindset.

What follows are less well-known techniques, but they are nevertheless effective ways to turn anxiety on its head and see the world from a completely different angle. Think of anxiety as nothing more than a "spin" on reality—you can just as easily change the narrative in another direction that makes you feel happier, more relaxed, and more confident in yourself. Let's look at how.

6. ACCEPT YOUR ANXIETY

The poet Robert Frost once wrote, "The only way out is through."

He could have been writing about anxiety!

If you suffer from social anxieties, overthinking, or excessive stress and worry, your mindset may be something like: "This is wrong, and I need to get rid of it." Maybe we imagine a silver bullet or some kind of overnight insight that will fix us forever. And given how difficult it can be to live with anxiety, it's not very satisfying to be told to just "accept" it.

But a big part of how anxiety works is that it is a reinforcing chain reaction. Let's say you become aware of something that doesn't feel quite right. You focus in on it, you start to imagine worse things, you notice yourself focusing on those worse things, and then before you know it, you're spiraling out of control. However, if we approach ourselves and our anxiety with judgment and resistance, we end up adding even more links to this chain reaction. The irony is that desperately trying to escape problems is just another way to focus on them . . . it's a way we give ourselves *another* problem!

The real way out of anxiety is not to push or pull, not to succumb to it or run screaming from it. It's simply to sit calmly with how you actually feel.

People can mistakenly think that acceptance means we agree with what's happening, or that we like it. We might think that acceptance means we take no responsibility for getting better. This isn't true. Acceptance just means we plainly acknowledge the fact of what is, *without struggle.* It's this absence of struggle that gives us the freedom we want.

And we can have that feeling of freedom even though we still occasionally suffer from anxiety!

An attitude of acceptance tells us that:

- It's not the end of the world to feel anxious.
- It's human to feel that way, and many other people do.
- There's nothing to be ashamed of.
- We are not weak, crazy, or failures because we are stressed or having a hard time.
- Anxiety is unpleasant, but it won't kill us.
- Thoughts are just thoughts.

- It's normal and perfectly okay to feel anxious or worried sometimes.
- We can feel anxiety and still live happy, effective, and full lives.
- It is not possible to be completely free of anxiety—but it is possible to learn to live a happy life with a certain degree of anxiety.

This last one is important. Sometimes, if we expect that our treatment or self-improvement goals are met to perfection, it can inspire us to give up when we feel we've failed to meet these ideals. But our goal should not be perfection, absolute control, and zero percent anxiety. Our goal is simply to be more accepting, tolerant, and compassionate about who we are, good and bad.

That's why the best way to manage anxiety is not to push against it, run away, fight it, judge it, or avoid it . . . but to simply accept it. The more we fight our thoughts, the stronger they become—especially when those thoughts are anxious in nature. But when you let them pass, they calmly fade away.

Anxiety can be thought of as your brain's mistaken attempt to maintain control. Overthinking feels like problem-solving, but it isn't. To fully accept your anxiety is to let go of this illusion of control and give up churning things over in your head in a way that has no effect on your world except to make you unhappy.

One great way to start practicing more acceptance is to closely watch our self-talk. Watch closely for emotionally loaded, extreme black-and-white thinking, such as beliefs about "always," "never," or "everybody." If you say to yourself, "I have to get this right or else," then stop and consider whether you really *have to*. Is it really, truly a nonnegotiable that you get it right? Will the whole world end if you don't get it right?

A big one is, "I can't handle this." This is basically an instruction to your brain, saying: it's an emergency, you're in a dangerous situation, and you can do nothing about it. Pretty anxiety-provoking, right? It's also very, very seldomly true. Tone it down and change the thought to, "This will be challenging, but I can get through it," or, "Just because I'm feeling anxious now doesn't mean that things won't work out."

The trick here, as you can see, is not to convince yourself that the danger isn't there and that you don't feel anxious. You do! But what happens when you look at that anxiety and say to it, "Fine, no big deal. I see you. It's okay that you're here." Sometimes we can't do much to get rid of our anxious feelings, but we can change the way we interpret that anxiety. This is what acceptance is. You had a panic attack last night? Okay. It happens. People sometimes get anxiety attacks, and you got one last night. Everything is okay now, though. Even if it does happen again, you'll manage it."

If you can do this, you'll realize that fighting anxious feelings is actually half of your anxiety in the first place! If you had a painful spasm in one of your muscles, you wouldn't try to fix it with brute force, right? That would just make the problem worse. In the same way, let yourself off the hook and let go of being anxious about anxiety.

Here's a quick exercise the next time you're feeling anxious: talk to your amygdala. This part of your brain evolved for good reason. The fear response is a gift that keeps us safe and alive. It's a *good* thing that the amygdala can move quicker than our rational brain because in life-or-death moments, every split-second counts.

However, the amygdala is just a part of your body. And it can be wrong! We can stop, take a breath, and ask our higher brain to weigh in. We can challenge our thought processes, become aware of what we're doing, and consciously choose what we want to do. The next time you're feeling stressed and overwhelmed, say in your mind, "Thank you, amygdala, for bringing my attention to this. Thanks for trying to keep me safe. My higher brain can take it from here, though!"

It's not that our knee-jerk fight-or-flight response is *wrong* or that we are to blame for being triggered into a cycle of overthinking and rumination. It's simply a misfire. Seeing your reactions this way takes the angst out of them. Anxiety, then, is a bit like having an allergic reaction or getting indigestion—it's uncomfortable, yes, but not the end of the world and not something you have to go to war with. It's not dangerous. It's not shameful. You haven't done anything wrong.

If you can literally visualize yourself thanking your amygdala and your stress response, then giving it permission to stand down, then you take the power away from that anxiety. You realize that just because your amygdala is going crazy, it doesn't mean you have to respond or that you are under its control.

7. TELL YOURSELF YOU'RE JUST EXCITED

As you can see, perspective is everything. Anxiety and stress are facts of life, but so much of how they feel comes down to how we *frame* that anxiety and stress. In other words, instead of trying to tackle anxiety, start by telling yourself that you are not actually experiencing anxiety at all.

Let's take a look at this word "anxious." When you diagnose your state of mind with this word, the next steps are clear—you want to mitigate the anxiety, fix it, escape it, accept it, or deal with it somehow. But let's take a step back and consider whether our appraisal of "anxiety" is even accurate.

Physiologically, anxiety is actually arousal—our autonomic nervous system is activated, and we are on high alert. But in truth, there is nothing especially wrong with this state of mind—unless we convince ourselves there is. After all, physiological arousal also happens when we're stimulated, excited, thrilled, or inspired. This is why some people can look at jumping out of an airplane as a catastrophically scary event, while others may see it as exhilarating. The body response is the same—only the narrative about what those sensations mean changes.

One way to deal with anxiety is to try to relax ourselves. That's a good strategy. But another strategy is to ask, "Hang on a second, is the way I'm feeling really so bad?" A study by Dr. Alison Wood Brooks found that eighty-five percent of questionnaire participants said they thought the best thing to do with anxiety was to relax. But as we all know, "just relax" is easier said than done! What if instead you said, "I'm not anxious, I'm just excited"? You don't have to change anything.

When you reframe, you're already where you need to be.

Maybe it's a *good* thing that you feel a little stressed being outside your comfort zone—it shows you're growing. For example, if you feel anxious that you have "imposter syndrome," you could reframe the experience. Isn't feeling a little anxious part of the learning process? If it seems like too much of a leap to say you're excited, say, "I'm looking forward to being excited," or, "Well, this is interesting!" Just a subtle switch from fear and resistance to curiosity can make all the difference.

Dr. Brooks also did some fascinating experiments. She surprised study participants with some moderately anxiety-inducing tasks—one of which was to sing a song ("Don't Stop Believin'" by Journey, if you're interested). Participants were told to say either, "I'm anxious," or, "I'm excited." The group who said they were excited actually felt more excited and sang better as measured by a machine that records pitch and volume. The same thing happened when other participants were tasked with giving a speech to a camera. The "excited" group was measured objectively as more persuasive and confident.

Here's the interesting part-in each case, both groups showed the same amount of anxiety. Their heart rates were the same; their cortisol levels were the same. But by simply using this word "excited," they put themselves in an **opportunity** mindset rather than a **threat** mindset. And so, they felt better and performed better.

It might not feel very natural to claim how enthusiastic you are about everything, but just try it. You will get better with a little practice. And as with so many other reframing and perspective-switching exercises, you don't have to one hundred percent believe what you're saying, either. You may benefit simply from *not* saying that you're anxious.

So, there are three main ways to deal with anxiety:
1. Emotional suppression
2. Emotional regulation or acceptance
3. Emotional reappraisal

A 2009 study in *Behavior Research and Therapy* by Hoffman and colleagues has suggested that reappraisal and acceptance are more effective than trying to suppress anxiety. In their research, they asked 202 participants in three groups to give an impromptu filmed speech. The first group was the reappraisal group, the second the suppression group, and the third the acceptance group, according to how they were told to approach their anxiety. The suppression group actually ended up increasing their heart rates and worsening their anxiety.

"However," the researchers concluded, "the acceptance and suppression groups did not differ in their subjective anxiety response. These results suggest that both reappraising and accepting anxiety is more effective for moderating the physiological arousal than suppressing anxiety. However, **reappraising is more effective for moderating the subjective feeling of anxiety** than attempts to suppress or accept it."

To practice this kind of reframing in your own life, you need only make a conscious effort to remove words like "stressed," "worried," anxious," and so on from your vocabulary. Instead, talk about opportunities, chances, excitement, enthusiasm, interest, or even just novelty. You'll see just how easy it is to convince your body that the butterflies in your stomach are a pleasant sensation!

Before we end this chapter, it's worth considering one more point about the power of reappraisal. Your body's stress response evolved over millions of years because it successfully helped your ancestors survive genuine threats in the environment. In other words, panic and anxiety do serve a purpose, even though in modern day life we seldom face the kind of survival threats this system originally evolved to detect. However, in the mean time we have also developed a powerful higher brain that endows us with the ability to reflect, reason logically, and plan.

What all this means is that we can change the attitude we hold towards ingrained feelings of fear and panic. Many sufferers of anxiety tend to believe that if they feel anxious, then there is only one way to respond. For example, if they feel afraid to do something, then they shouldn't do it. If it feels scary, then it should be avoided. If something feels bad, it is bad, and so on.

But you can reappraise what anxiety *means* to you entirely. Too often we assume that if we find something anxiety-inducing it means we need to stay away from that thing, or do whatever we can to get rid of the bad feeling. But what if we told ourselves that anxiety simply has no bearing on what we choose to do or not do?

This is the deeper philosophy behind "feel the fear and do it anyway." If you fully expect and anticipate a bit of anxiety when attempting something new or going out of your comfort zone, then you are not surprised by it, and you never grant it the power to stop you or stand in your way. When you realize that you are always able to act according to your goals and values, *whether you are anxious or not*, the anxiety loses its power over you.

8. WRITE TO YOUR FUTURE SELF

One creative way to gain perspective on your anxiety is "future journaling" or writing notes to your future self. Anxiety tends to narrow perspective. As we've already seen, we can be horrible judges of reality when we're hyper focused on some perceived problem. But when we write a letter to our future selves, we broaden our vision.

Imagine you're stressing about the renovation of your new home, worried about money, and feeling overwhelmed by everything you need to do. Let's say you sit down and write a letter to ninety-year-old you. What do you say?

What will ultimately matter when you're that old, looking back on your life? Will you really care about having done everything perfectly, or will your memories be about how you worked hard to create a family home that you could fill with love?

Try this exercise when you're feeling swamped in a problem, and you'll be amazed at just how clarifying it is. It's funny how a little distance can help dissolve all the nonsense of life and help us see our deepest values more clearly. You can future journal to yourself in two weeks or in twenty years. You can confide in and share worries with your older, wiser self, and even imagine what that self would tell you in return.

Almost always, your older self *wouldn't* say, "I think you're not anxious enough—you should worry more!"

When you future journal, let your thoughts wander a little.

What does the ideal resolution to the current challenge look like?

Why does this challenge bother you so much?

What would a good friend advise you to do in this situation?

What's really important here . . . and what isn't?

What will happen here if things don't go to plan?

What good things in this situation have you been discounting?

What bad things have you focused on in this situation?

How would you look back on this current situation, being older and wiser?

That's not all, though. After you've written the letter, come back to it later. Did the thing you were so anxious about come to pass? And if it did, was your reaction what you thought it would be? Was it as bad as you predicted?

When you're in the grip of anxiety, you can start to take your own fears and assumptions as gospel. But when you get a broader view across time, you realize, with some relief, that you're often just plain wrong. What you thought was a big deal in May turns out to be forgotten completely in June. What you thought you wanted turned out not to be the thing you needed, and so on. So, the next time you're in a panic about something, you can pause and remember that your assessment just might be inaccurate.

In a study published in the *Journal of Experimental Psychology*, Dr. Kitty Klein and colleagues asked seventy-one students to do three twenty-minute expressive writing exercises over a period of two weeks. "The results suggest that the simple act of writing about stressful events can have a positive impact on academic performance—although for how long remains unknown," concluded the authors. When we combine this expressive writing with a long-range view into the future, we gain a few insights:

- How we feel today is not how we'll feel tomorrow
- We are not always accurate in our predictions about the future
- Though transitions and challenges can be difficult, we have coped before and will cope again
- In the future, we may possess new information, skills and abilities that we don't possess now

Future journaling is something you can incorporate into a regular journal-writing habit, or you can try it out specifically when you're having a hard time. Keep track of goals by writing a letter to a future self after the time you expect to achieve that goal. Have you achieved what you wanted? If not, what does that look like? Are you happy? What did you do next? What did you learn, and how did you overcome your challenges?

You can just ask your future self these questions without needing to answer them. Simply allow the questions to clarify and condense your own position in the present. If you like, you can combine this exercise with a visualization session—try to imagine your future self. Alternatively, talk to your future self mentally and do a role-play. What would you learn if you interviewed your future self about the current problem you're facing?

You could use these letters to rehearse different outcomes and see how you feel about them. Imagine that everything goes "wrong" and that what you're worried about comes to pass. What does that actually look like for your future self? Is it that bad? Most problems shrink down to nothing when you consider whether you'll actually care about them in a year's time.

If you're on the cusp of making a decision, slow down and consult with your future self. What would *they* think of your choice? Try to be reasonable and rational. Don't leap into anything new until you've taken the longer view. One fun thing to do is to write yourself an email and schedule to have it delivered to you on a set date in the future. Or write yourself a letter on every birthday to read in one year's time. The act of seeing where you were a year ago and forecasting where you'll be a year from now is a powerful and grounding practice.

What's great is that over time, you will collect and amazing collage of letters written across a longer and longer time span. Not only will you see broader themes gradually emerging, you'll also notice that with space and distance, life's greatest challenges often seem to deliver the most valuable lessons, and that in hindsight, considering your entire life as a whole, you can start to bring enormous gratitude and compassion to the "big picture" of your time on this earth. In the same way as we may love a novel and all the events that happen in it, good or bad, we start to appreciate everything that we experience, good or bad, because it's part of an enormous, fascinating story that is not finished being told yet!

Finally, a variation on this exercise is to write a letter to a future anxious self when you're currently feeling strong and happy. Write from your calm, content point of view. What would you like to tell your future stressed-out self? When you're in the grips of stress and anxiety, it's so hard to pull yourself out of it, but if you can get a glimpse of yourself in a happier state of mind, you remind yourself that not only is it possible to feel that way, but that it's likely! "Dear stressed future self, I know things look pretty rough right now, but you actually have a great life with a lot to be thankful for. You know how it is; you struggle for a few days, but you always find your way through . . ." Think of it as a greeting card from better days—"wish you were here!"

9. LEARN HOW TO SAY "I DON'T"

This trick is for all those people whose anxiety and stress comes from being a people-pleaser or not knowing how to say no. Sometimes, the best way to manage stress is to set up stronger boundaries so that we don't take on more than we can handle. Saying *no* can be hard for some people, but with a simple switch in perspective, we can see that it's about saying *yes* to what really matters to you. This then becomes a question of values, goals and priorities, and not merely one of boundaries.

Everyone finds turning people down a little awkward, but if this is a weak point for you, thankfully there are some scientifically proven ways to best say no. First things first, change your perspective:

Saying no is a healthy, normal thing to do. You don't have endless resources or time (none of us do!), and so you have to prioritize certain things over others. It's just a fact of life, and having to disappoint people now and then is *not* a sign that you're doing something wrong or are a bad person. Saying no helps you shape your life according to your values, and you are not required to say yes out of guilt or obligation to others. In fact, saying yes to everything not only creates stress for you, but it's seldom the favor to others we think it is!

Well, now that that's out of the way, let's consider the most effective method for saying no. Obviously, you don't want to be rude, hurt people's feelings or create more problems for yourself. But you also don't want to be unclear or end up over-compromising. So, what do you do?

In a research study published in the *Journal of Consumer Research*, 120 participants were divided into two groups, one group saying, "I can't," when turning down a request, and the other saying, "I don't." For example, turning down a tempting treat of ice cream could be done with "I can't eat ice cream," or, "I don't eat ice cream."

Afterward, the participants answered some unrelated questions. They then thought the study was over, but it wasn't. As they were leaving, each participant was offered a chocolate bar or healthy granola bar. The results? Those who were told to say "I can't" earlier ate the unhealthy chocolate bar sixty-one percent of the time. Those who said "I don't" only ate the unhealthy chocolate bar thirty-six percent of the time!

The same researchers designed another similar study, inviting thirty women to a "wellness" seminar and dividing them into three groups. After being asked about their long-term health goals, one group was told to "just say no" to temptations, the second group was told to use "I can't" language, and the third to say, "I don't." Only three out of ten of the "just say no" group were able to persist with their goal throughout the ten-day seminar. The "I can't" group only managed one woman out of ten who stuck to her goal. And the "I don't" group fared best of all, with an impressive eight out of ten women achieving what they set out to.

Granted, this study focused on self-discipline and goal setting, but the principles also apply to establishing and maintaining boundaries. This is because "I don't" language is all about control and empowerment. We tell ourselves that we're the kind of people who follow certain values. It's an inborn trait rather than something imposed on us from the outside (doesn't "I can't" just make you think of someone passively following a rule someone else set for them?).

I don't is a choice freely made and immovable. It's almost phrased as a law of the universe.

I can't is an external limitation, an excuse—and it invites resistance! People may want to jump in and suggest ways that you factually *can* do what's requested.

Take a look:

"Hey, can you look after my nine obnoxious bulldogs this weekend at short notice?"

"Oh, I'm sorry, I can't! I'm, uh, having guests over that weekend."

"Oh, no problem, they won't be any trouble. Your guests will love them!"

"Hmm, I don't know... I think I just, uh, remembered that one of them is allergic to dogs!"

"Oh, don't worry about that, it'll be fine. They make medication for that now."

Compare this to:

"Hey, can you look after my nine obnoxious bulldogs this weekend at short notice?"

"Oh, I'm sorry, but no. I don't have dogs in my house, I'm afraid!"

"Oh. Well, that's a shame."

When you say no the right way, it's not in order to get the other person to really believe it; it's to make sure that *you* really believe it and communicate that sureness clearly. It's a skill to say no and really mean it. Keep your no:

1. Short
2. Firm
3. Polite

Remember that your phrasing, tone, expression, and body language should all be communicating the fact that your no is really final and decided, as though it really were a law of nature and *not* something to be negotiated. If they ask again, simply say no again without feeling like you have to do something else to appease them or apologize for not acquiescing. There's no need to add any extra information or apologize. Don't jump in to solve a problem or beat yourself up for not being more accommodating. Just say no (you don't even have to give a reason) and smile politely.

If you feel like you've been caught off guard with a request, a great tip is to say, "Let me just think about that and I'll get back to you soon." This buys you time to think clearly through your wants and needs and your practical limitations. Do you really want to do it? Plan your response (try a role-play or rehearsal!) and then be assertive, but polite, if you say no.

It always pays to be polite, but do so in a way that doesn't leave you open to "negotiation." If you say things like, "Oh I wish I could, but I can't," you are actually inviting the same request later. People may hear the first part ("I wish") and not the second part ("I can't") and assume that you want them to persuade you.

Finally, don't forget that you can always give a modified yes.

"Could you finish this report this evening before you go home?"

"No, that's going to be a big rush, I'm afraid. I can complete it for you tomorrow afternoon if you're willing to wait?"

What you are doing here is saying yes – to what you can and want to say yes to. As always, focus and framing matters, and if you frame your response so as to draw attention to everything you *are* willing to do, then the entire conversation shifts away from all the things you aren't willing to do.

Saying "no" properly may not seem like it has much to do with to anxiety and stress, but a well-made refusal is often a way to draw a boundary against stress and worry *before* it has time to get into our heads and take up residence there. If you're feeling anxious about commitments, tasks, and obligations, ask yourself honestly how much of what's in your head belongs there in the first place. It may be that half your stress and worry could be avoided by saying no earlier on.

Ultimately, time, resource, and energy management is intimately connected with stress management. It may feel awkward at first to be more assertive, but remember that a polite no is actually an act of respect—for yourself and for the other person.

10. HAVE NO OPINION

Let's end our book with a simple, but effective, attitude to hold when it comes to the stress and anxiety of life. In the words of famous Stoic philosopher Marcus Aurelius, "You always own the option of having no opinion. There is never any need to get worked up or to trouble your soul about things you can't control. These things are not asking to be judged by you. Leave them alone."

For overthinkers and ruminators, truly grasping this sentiment can be a life-changer. It's akin to the sudden insight that most (all?) of our rumination is *100% optional*. In a world where seemingly everyone has to have an opinion about everything (usually, a forceful opinion), it can be a welcome relief to remember that opinions are actually optional. You don't *need* to go in and make a pronouncement or judgment about every little thing that comes your way. It's simple, but easy to forget: having an "opinion" about something that we cannot change and are not responsible for is a perfect way to invite dissatisfaction and anxiety into our lives. But we can always choose to leave them alone.

You don't have to be a fixer.
You don't have to decide who is right or wrong.
You don't have to agree or disagree.
You don't have to engage at all, in fact.

So often, this kind of engagement comes with anxiety, especially if we are getting tangled up in things that are not really our business. For example, you scroll through social media and discover a post that you can tell has been designed to polarize people. There's a goodie, there's a baddie, and you're being invited to harshly condemn or mock the baddie. How many times have you taken the bait and gotten worked up about this kind of thing?

Suddenly, people and issues and ideas that you hadn't heard of a moment before fill your brain, and you immediately jump in to decide what you think about it. In fact, you may even consider it some kind of duty to pick which side you fall on and why. It may feel like getting outraged is the righteous, noble thing to do. This knee-jerk reaction can be so swift that you never even stop to consider if you *want* to get involved with it in the first place.

Let's consider another example. You've messed up at work and you're feeling completely stressed out about how you're going to save face and how you're going to make it up to people. You ruminate endlessly about it. It's as though your brain wants to answer the question: "Just how bad are you?" Sometimes you get defensive and feel like blaming other people; other times you're filled with embarrassment about what you've done and feel really bad.

But who says you have to play this game at all? Is it really necessary to find out who's to blame and just how much they are to blame in order for you to carry on? You can take your steps to address the situation without getting emotionally involved at all.

The Stoics were fans of serenity and the emotional regulation that comes with letting go of what really isn't in your control. Does having an opinion improve your life? If you're honest, the most likely answer is "no." And considering that "opinions" often come with a dose of confusion, anxiety, stress, and obligation, why not just drop them? There are a million problems out there in the world, and always will be. But none of them are asking you to have an opinion of them. What's more, you having an opinion is not necessary for you to be happy, to be effective, or to act toward your goals. What freedom!

There's another way we can interpret Aurelius' quote: we can always delay our opinion if we must have one. In the face of uncertainty or confusion, we can learn to comfortably say, "I don't know," or "I'll make a decision . . . but just not yet." This is not a sign of weakness, laziness, or rudeness. It does not mean we're unintelligent. It certainly doesn't undermine in any way the decision we may ultimately come to. In fact, it may add more gravitas to that decision.

Stress and anxiety go hand in hand with rushing. But when it comes to the most important things in life, you don't have to rush. Be okay with letting the moment be unclear, unknowable, or in process. You can act later. You can choose not to act at all. No matter how fraught and stressful things may feel, you always retain that option.

Summary:

- We are always at liberty to reframe our anxiety and look at things in different ways. One way to do this is to consciously practice acceptance of how we feel, rather than always trying to escape it, fix it, or judge it. This doesn't mean we agree with it or don't want to be better; it just means we relinquish the struggle.
- By simply saying, "I'm excited," instead of, "I'm anxious," we open a different perspective that helps us interpret the same physiological arousal as less threatening, helping us perform better.
- Try writing to your future self to gain deep perspective and remind yourself of what ultimately matters. Ask for advice from a wiser, older version of yourself, or write a note from your calm self to your stressed self, offering advice.

- Stress management is often time management and knowing how to say no to too many commitments. Be short, firm, and polite and say, "I don't," instead of, "I can't," if you want people to respect that boundary.
- Finally, take Aurelius' advice and remember that you always have the option to have no opinion. You don't have to judge, decide, agree, or take sides. And if you must, realize that you can always postpone your judgment.

CHAPTER 1. YOUR ANXIETY MANAGEMENT TOOLKIT

- Whatever form stress and anxiety take in your life, it's worth having some psychological tools to help you manage it mindfully. Build more self-awareness by learning to label your emotions and noting how they feel on your body in the moment. We can also build self-awareness by keeping a regular thought diary, or by taking psychometric tests.

- We don't have to accept our anxious thoughts as gospel. The Socratic questioning method asks us to look for evidence, become curious, and deliberately seek out alternative interpretations. We can likewise test our false beliefs by reappraising our assessment of the situation and the "threat" we see.

- Making a mind map gives us perspective and clarity on the chaos that may be in our minds. Start with a single word or phrase and do a "brain dump," then look for patterns and themes, asking what you can control and what you cannot. One of the best cures for anxiety is to ask what you can realistically **do** about your situation.

- The ABC model helps us understand the antecedents, beliefs, and consequences of our stress reaction, and allows us to re-engineer our perspective and behave differently.
- One option is to simply distract yourself by giving your brain an engaging "mind game."

CHAPTER 2. AN ANXIETY-FREE LIFESTYLE

- Easy, everyday lifestyle changes can make a big difference with anxiety and overthinking. An obvious area to examine is whether you're having too much caffeine. Try to limit yourself to four hundred milligrams daily.
- Everyone worries, so at least do it strategically by scheduling worry time. Keep a worry journal so that instead of fighting worry, you postpone and contain it, tackling it on your own terms.
- Practice gratitude daily to gently shift your perspective to focus on everything that is going well in your world. Use a journal or

write thank-you notes to people who have shown you kindness.

- Mental anchoring is a technique that, once established, can be used as often as you like to help ground and calm you. Choose an anchor, choose a desired state, then connect the two during visualization so that revisiting the anchor brings you back to that state of mind.
- Have a consistent morning routine where you focus on good food, nature, healthy habits, and quiet contemplative time where you set your intention for the day. Make sure you're hydrated, since dehydration can elevate cortisol levels.
- Finally, choose a hobby that can act as a pleasant distraction—but make sure you're choosing something you genuinely enjoy.

CHAPTER 3. ENTER YOUR MIND

- Mindfulness techniques are a proven and effective way to combat anxiety, stress, and overthinking, but you don't have to do formal sitting meditation to get the benefits.

- One easy technique is to take a few minutes to practice deep belly breathing to oxygenate and relax your body.
- Another is to use the 5-4-3-2-1 grounding technique to come back into your body and the present moment by tuning into all five senses. You could finish by seeking out something positive about the situation or yourself.
- Chanting a mantra is another accessible mindfulness technique. Try saying an affirmation aloud or just internally to distract and calm yourself.
- Do a body scan in the morning to check in with how you're feeling and correct any minor tensions before they become strong negative emotions and anxious thoughts. Use the CALM acronym to scan Chest, Arms, Legs, and Mouth, scan from head to toe, or simply ask your body what it wants to communicate to you. Use progressive muscle relaxation to loosen any tension you find.
- Laughter meditation takes a little bravery, but can flood you with feel-good hormones and banish stress and anxiety, whether practiced alone or in a group.
- Try loving kindness meditation to calm social anxiety, and learn to be a little kinder and compassionate with yourself.

CHAPTER 4. THE FIRST STEP IS SEEING IT

- The imagination is a powerful thing and can be put to use to help combat anxiety and quell overthinking. Guided imagery, for example, is a great way to imagine a peaceful scenario in enough detail that our body responds by relaxing.

- Another effective stress management technique is to use metaphors to help you alter your relationship to anxiety and think of it in a different way. You could imagine that stress is like clouds passing by in the sky, passing trains, or a restless toddler.

- You can also gain this psychological distance by talking about yourself and your anxiety in the third person (for example, "David is worried about this" when talking about yourself).

- Role-play exercises are another way to use the power of visualizing. Literally act out and rehearse anxiety-provoking scenarios with a friend or therapist, or try to practice situations in your mind to de-sensitize you and help you feel more prepared and confident.

- Finally, create an alter ego for yourself who possesses the opposite of some stressful characteristics you want to be free of. Flesh out this alter ego and allow yourself to take on their perspective as your own when you're faced with a challenging or stressful situation.

CHAPTER 5. REFRAME AND SHIFT

- We are always at liberty to reframe our anxiety and look at things in different ways. One way to do this is to consciously practice acceptance of how we feel rather than always trying to escape it, fix it, or judge it. This doesn't mean we agree with it or don't want to be better; it just means we relinquish the struggle.
- Simply saying, "I'm excited," instead of, "I'm anxious," opens us to a different perspective and helps us interpret the same physiological arousal as less threatening, helping us perform better.
- Try writing to your future self to gain deep perspective and remind yourself of what ultimately matters. Ask for advice from a wiser, older version of yourself, or write a

note from your calm self to your stressed self, offering advice.

- Stress management is often time management and knowing how to say no to too many commitments. Be short, firm, and polite and say, "I don't," instead of, "I can't," if you want people to respect that boundary.
- Finally, take Aurelius' advice and remember that you always have the option to have no opinion. You don't have to judge, decide, agree, or take sides. And if you must, realize that you can always postpone your judgment.

Printed in Great Britain
by Amazon